TIDE
OF WAR

Also by David R. Petriello

American Prometheus
Don't Give up the Soil
Military History of New Jersey
The Days of Heroes are Over
A Pestilence on Pennsylvania Avenue
Bacteria and Bayonets

TIDE
OF WAR

THE IMPACT OF
WEATHER ON WARFARE

DAVID R. PETRIELLO

Skyhorse Publishing

To my Guinevere, the only thing more powerful than nature and more eternal than the heavens is my love for you.

Skyhorse Publishing books may be purchased in bulk at special discounts for sales promotion, corporate gifts, fund-raising, or educational purposes. Special editions can also be created to specifications. For details, contact the Special Sales Department, Skyhorse Publishing, 307 West 36th Street, 11th Floor, New York, NY 10018 or info@skyhorsepublishing.com.

Skyhorse® and Skyhorse Publishing® are registered trademarks of Skyhorse Publishing, Inc.®, a Delaware corporation.

Visit our website at www.skyhorsepublishing.com.

10 9 8 7 6 5 4 3 2 1

Library of Congress Cataloging-in-Publication Data is available on file.

Cover design by Rain Saukas

Print ISBN: 978-1-5107-2819-6
Ebook ISBN: 978-1-5107-2821-9

Printed in the United States of America

CONTENTS

INTRODUCTION

If you know Heaven and you know Earth,
you make your victory complete.
—Sun Tzu

Much has been made in literature of whether war is a science or an art. Is it simply the correct application of figures and statistics in a formulistic way to achieve a desired result, or are there too many unexplainable and unquantifiable variables? Perhaps, as with many other things, the answer lies somewhere in the middle. While we may be able to observe and predict some elements of war, others are beyond the study or control of generals and strategists, with weather and nature being in this last category.

The British historian, Sir Edward Shepherd Creasy, wrote one of the first books on pivotal battles in world history in 1851. It is telling that of the fifteen battles he chose for his work, thirteen, including Marathon, Syracuse, Gaugamela, Teutoburg, Châlons, Tours, Hastings, Calais, Blenheim, Poltava, Saratoga, Valmy, and Waterloo, were heavily impacted by weather events. In fact, meteorological conditions that favored one side seem to be the only constant among the various engagements. Even Lt. Col. Joseph B. Mitchell's updated version of Creasy's work, which features five additional nineteenth and twentieth century battles, includes at least four that were impacted by weather.

Weather, climate, and astronomical occurrences have influenced the waging of war by man since prehistory. Halley's Comet helped to announce the fall of the Shang Dynasty in China, a solar eclipse frightened the Macedonian army enough at Pydna in 168 BC to ensure victory for the Romans, a massive rain storm turned the field of Agincourt to mud in 1415 and gave Henry V his legendary victory, fog secured the throne of England for Edward IV at Barnet in 1471, wind and disease conspired to wreck the Spanish Armada, snow served to prevent the American capture of Quebec in 1775 and confined the Revolution to the Thirteen Colonies, excessive heat gave rise to the legend of Saladin at the Horns of Hattin in 1187, freezing cold nearly stopped Washington's crossing of the Delaware, and an earthquake helped to spark the Peloponnesian War. These serve as only a small portion of the many instances where nature has tipped the balance in combat.

Due to a combination of its destructive potential and unpredictable occurrence, the impact of nature has worried both common people and military commanders from ancient times to the present. It is perhaps not surprising then that many of the chief gods of ancient man involved some element of weather within their bailiwick, such as Jupiter, Zeus, Indra, Ba'al, and Horus. Many of these were at the same time gods of war as well, including the latter three. Numerous other cultures had additional, lesser deities who represented both weather and warfare, notably Theispas of Urartu, Tlaloc of the Aztec, Tohil of the Maya, Shala of Sumer, and the Norse god Thor. Man's agricultural revolution had much to do with this, as weather was often the determining factor between years of plenty and years of starvation and ruin. Thus, more agricultural civilizations tended to worship chief gods who connected to farming while pastoral or nomadic people worshipped deities of various other elements, such as Tengri of the Mongols or Igaluk of the Inuit who represented the sky and moon respectively.

This close association between a successful control of the environment and victory in war is clearly seen in one of the most important Greek myths. As retold by Hesiod in his *Theogony*, the Titanomachy was a ten-year-long war between Zeus and the Olympians against Cronus and the Titans. Zeus's acquisition of lightning—allowing him to control nature and defeat his father in battle—finally led Zeus's upstart faction to victory over his father.

> Then Zeus no longer held back his might; but straight his heart was filled with fury and he showed forth all his strength. From Heaven and from Olympus he came forthwith, hurling his lightning: The bold flew thick and fast from his strong hand together with thunder and lightning, whirling an awesome flame. The life-giving earth crashed around in burning, and the vast wood crackled loud with fire all about. All the land seethed, and Ocean's streams and the unfruitful sea. The hot vapor lapped round the earthborn Titans: Flame unspeakable rose to the bright upper air: The flashing glare of the thunder-stone and lightning blinded their eyes for all that there were strong. Astounding heat seized Chaos: And to see with eyes and to hear the sound with ears it seemed even as if Earth and wide Heaven above came together; for such a mighty crash would have arisen if Earth were being hurled to ruin, and Heaven from on high were hurling her down; so great a crash was there while the gods were meeting together in strife. Also the winds brought rumbling earthquake and dust storm, thunder and lightning and the lurid thunderbolt, which are the shafts of great Zeus, and carried the clangor and the war cry into the midst of the two hosts. A horrible uproar of terrible strife arose: Mighty deeds were shown and the battle inclined. But until then, they kept at one another and fought continually in cruel war.[1]

Shortly afterward, the new inhabitants of Mt. Olympus became involved in an even greater struggle. Gaia, out of anger due to the treatment of the giants, gave birth to the monster, Typhon.

> Strength was with his hands in all that he did and the feet of the
> strong god were untiring. From his shoulders grew a hundred heads
> of a snake, a fearful dragon, with dark, flickering tongues, and from
> under the brows of his eyes in his marvelous heads flashed fire, and
> fire burned from his heads as he glared. And there were voices in all
> his dreadful heads which uttered every kind of sound unspeakable;
> for at one time they made sounds such that the gods understood,
> but at another, the noise of a bull bellowing aloud in proud ungov-
> ernable fury; and at another, the sound of a lion, relentless of heart;
> and at another's, sounds like whelps, wonderful to hear; and again, at
> another, he would hiss, so that the high mountains re-echoed.[2]

Though various versions of the story exist, in all Zeus once again relied
upon his power over the forces of nature to defeat the enemy.

> And through the two of them heat took hold on the dark-blue sea,
> through the thunder and lightning, and through the fire from the
> monster, and the scorching winds and blazing thunderbolt. The
> whole earth seethed, and sky and sea: and the long waves raged along
> the beaches round and about, at the rush of the deathless gods: and
> there arose an endless shaking.[3]

Nor was the idea of nature interacting with world affairs limited to the
West. The Indian classic, the *Mahabharata*, mentions a number of nat-
ural and climatic occurrences that portended disaster in the upcoming
Kurukshetra War, a legendary conflict in Vedic literature.

> Strong winds are blowing fiercely and the dust ceaseth not. The earth
> is frequently trembling, and *Rahu* approacheth towards the sun. The
> white planet (*Ketu*) stayeth, having passed beyond the constellation
> *Chitra*. All this particularly bodeth the destruction of the Kurus. A
> fierce comet riseth, afflicting the constellation *Pusya*. This great planet
> will cause frightful mischief to both the armies.[4]

Nature affecting war was a universal human archetype.

The many variables and unknowns of warfare have been best described by the expression "fog of war," after the following pronouncement by Clausewitz: "War is the realm of uncertainty; three quarters of the factors on which action in war is based are wrapped in a fog of greater or lesser uncertainty. A sensitive and discriminating judgment is called for; a skilled intelligence to scent out the truth." It is perhaps telling that this great theorist used a meteorological term to designate the unknown in war. Even as warfare became more professional and more of a science following the Enlightenment, weather remained an understood, but still often unpredictable component of fighting.

Over the past four thousand years, weather and nature have both hindered and helped various campaigns and battles, occasionally even altering the course of history in the process. In this vein it closely parallels the military history of disease, as both tended to be unpredictable and uncontrollable elements. Similarly, as technology and knowledge advanced, man's understanding and control over both reached a point of, while not immunity, at least partial resistance. Today both pestilence and the elements of nature still affect the planning and waging of war, and yet they are variables that can be accounted for to some extent. Yet, as with many other elements in the fog of war, nature is hardly a domesticated force and continues to unpredictably affect or predictably constrain combat around the world.

This book will trace some of the most notable intersections between nature and war since ancient times. It is broken into three main sections, corresponding to astronomical events, weather, and finally attempts to influence or control these events. We will examine each particular phenomenon in an attempt to demonstrate man's progress in both understanding and control up to the present day. While weather may not be the *sine qua non* of influences on victory in war, it is certainly a force to be both understood and studied.

1

COMETS

When beggars die there are no comets seen;
The heavens themselves blaze forth the death of princes.
—*JULIUS CAESAR*, ACT II, SCENE II, Lines 30–31

THE UNKNOWN THAT IS ASSOCIATED WITH the heavens has always scared man. Even long after the mechanics of eclipses was understood and the fear associated with them all but extinct, there still exists specters in outer space that stoke men's fear. The Solar System is hardly empty, nor is it only populated by nine planets traveling in predictable circuits around the Sun. Asteroids, comets, and countless other rogue bodies also inhabit the system, often moving in more erratic ways. The spectacular and devastating show provided by the Hale-Bopp Comet as it plunged into Jupiter in 1997 certainly awakened many to the possibility that this could also happen to our planet. While modern governments and their citizens have more recently become concerned about the vast amount of rogue material in space that could collide with Earth and cause untold devastation, the ancients were no less cognizant nor less afraid of these objects. Yet for premodern man the issue of meteoroids and comets was not one of terrestrial damage but of divine foreboding. For civilizations that built themselves on the predictability of nature, it was the unpredictable that inspired fear.

The ancient Greeks named the various planets of our solar system αστηρ πλανητης, or wandering stars, due to their seemingly nomadic nature. Yet, despite their apparently erratic paths, even these objects had a predictable pattern to their heavenly journeys. Every so often though, these early astronomers would find in the night sky an object that surpassed explanation. These truly wandering objects seemed to arrive from nowhere, blazed forth periodically across the sky, and then disappeared into the infinite. The Greeks referred to these as "long-haired stars," which came into the English language as "comets." Pliny, in his *Natural History*, summed up the ancient view of these, describing them as, "a very terrible portent."[5] Though clearly there is no scientific connection between the arrival of a comet and current events, primitive men nonetheless connected the two. For his part, Pliny associated a presumed sighting over Egypt in the tenth century BC with the aforementioned battle between Zeus and Typhon. "A terrible comet was seen by the people of Ethiopia and Egypt, to which Typhon, the king of that period gave his name."[6] Halfway across Asia at the site of another great river valley civilization, the Aryans likewise associated the appearance of "a fierce comet" with the legendary Kurukshetra War.[7]

Comets were a terrifying force, used by some to explain events after the fact and by others to portend the outcome of future undertakings. Much like the turtle shells used by the oracles of Shang Dynasty China or the livers that were studied by the haruspices of Etruria and Rome, augurs used the shape, color, and direction of comets to differentiate observations. Pliny himself recorded at least eleven different types, including bearded-stars, javelin-stars, dagger-stars, quoit-stars, tub-stars, horned-star, torch-star, horse-star, shining comet, goat comet, and mane-shaped.[8]

A brief survey of history will reveal that the sighting and reading of comets was not restricted to merely political events and questions, but military ones as well. In a similar vein, generals lucky, or sometimes unlucky, enough to observe a comet before battle could use its sighting to dictate the battle ahead. Again, much as with lay political observers, comets also entered discussion after the fact to explain the outcome of wars. Finally, it is certainly likely that much of the literature available on the proximity of comets to monumental battles in history is mere propaganda. Yet even myths and tall tales could serve to drive decisions for future generations who acted upon them or their advice.

The first comet to be mentioned in historical records with certainty appears to have passed over China in 613 BC during the reign of King Qing. The *Bamboo Annals* mention that, "in his sixth year, a comet entered the Great Bear; and the king died." Clearly, the chroniclers mentioned the astronomical occurrence due to this tragic event. Interestingly, an army of peasants defeated a superior chariot force, whose mission was to restore the ruler of Zi to power. As chariots were the elite units of the Chinese military at the time, this upset would have been just as jarring as the early demise of the monarch. It has been estimated that Halley's Comet was visible from Earth around October of 619 BC, making this observation a possible sighting.

Four hundred years before this event, astronomers estimate that Halley's Comet appeared over China around the year 1058 BC. While it was not recorded in any known Chinese text, the Shang Dynasty's well-known practices of astronomy and divination leave it safe to assume that they would have seen the powerful portent. The years around its appearance saw the initial outbreak of rebellion in the Zhou lands to the west of the capital as well as the descent into depravity of King Di Xin. It would be surprising if the Zhou did not use the comet in their well-documented propaganda efforts to attract the other feudal lords along the Yellow River. Shortly after this, the two sides engaged in the Battle of Muye, which resulted in the fall of the Shang and the rise of the Zhou for the next seven hundred years.

Likewise, Assyriologist George Smith wrote in the 1870s that when Nebuchadnezzar of Babylon invaded Elam, "an enormous comet appeared, the tail of which stretched, like a great reptile, from the north to the south of the heavens."[9] More recent research has shown that Halley's Comet did pass by Earth in April of 1142 BC.[10] Yet, this was most likely a generation before Nebuchadnezzar took the throne. Interestingly though, one of his predecessors, Marduk-kabit-ahheshu did reign during that decade and is also recorded as having pushed back the forces of Elam from Babylon, bringing about an end to the Kassite Dynasty. Perhaps the story was simply resurrected and reused for the subsequent conquest as well.

The first comet observed in the West to be connected to a battle occurred during perhaps the most trying war in Greek history, the second Persian invasion. Pliny reported that a "horned-star" appeared over Greece in 480 BC shortly before the Greeks were engaged in the Battle of Salamis.[11] Noah Webster, writing almost two thousand years later, connected the same comet to the outbreak of pestilence that crippled Xerxes's army as it was retreating back to Asia following that titanic loss.[12] It is interesting to note that neither Herodotus nor any more contemporaneous sources mention the appearance of the visitor in relation to the invasion.

Only fourteen years later, in 466 or 465 BC, sources report the appearance of two more heavenly visitors over the Greek homeland. The first appeared to the west and is said to have been visible at night for around eighty days beginning in June. Aristotle, in his *Meteorology*, connected its appearance with an earthquake in Achaea, perhaps the great Spartan earthquake that allegedly killed twenty thousand people and led to a revolt of the Helots.[13] In his work *On Religion*, Daimachus recorded that "for seventy five days continually, there was seen in the heavens a vast fiery body, as if it had been a flaming cloud, not resting, but carried about with several intricate and broken movements."[14] More recently, astronomers have speculated that this may have in fact been the first recorded appearance of Halley's Comet.[15] Another interesting connection, certainly not lost on the ancients, was that around that time occurred the Battle of the Eurymedon. Following the Second Persian War, the various Greek states had organized into a permanent alliance to both free Ionia and forestall a third invasion of Hellas. In 466 BC word reached the Greeks that a Persian fleet and army were forming near the Eurymedon River in southern Asia Minor. The Athenian general Cimon was dispatched with a fleet of two hundred Greek ships, catching the Persians by surprise and decimating their armada before it was completed. A comet seen in the western part of the sky could have certainly been interpreted as a western victory over an eastern foe.

Around this time, the philosopher Anaxagoras is said to have predicted that a piece of a heavenly body would break off and fall to Earth. Sure enough, a meteorite appears to have fallen only a month or so later, landing at Aegospotami in the Hellespont. "When it afterwards came down to the ground in this district, and the people of the place recovering from their fear and astonishment came together, there was no fire to be seen, neither any sign of it; there was only a stone lying, big indeed."[16] As with most objects of heavenly origin, something of a local cult emerged around the rock, a factor only augmented by the disastrous Battle of Aegospotami, fought there between Athens and Sparta in 405 BC.[17] Near the site of the meteor the Spartan fleet under Lysander destroyed the Athenian navy, bringing about the end of the Peloponnesian War. Plutarch records how, "some say the stone which fell down was a sign of this slaughter. For a stone of a great size did fall, according to the common belief, from heaven, at Aegospotami, which is shown to this day, and held in great esteem by the Chersonites."[18] Not surprisingly, ancient historians reported that a comet also visited at the outbreak of the Peloponnesian War between Athens and Sparta. Various histories, including Thucydides, record the sighting of a comet for upwards of sixty days in 431 BC, an event which was later taken to herald the commencement of the Peloponnesian War.

The cult that arose around the meteorite at Aegospotami was not unique, as numerous other examples populate human history, often connecting with military events. Some scientists and historians argue that one of the more famous meteorites is the black stone set in the Kaaba in Mecca. According to Islamic beliefs, the rock fell from Paradise as a sign to Adam and Eve. The Austrian scientist Paul Partsch expanded upon that idea in the 1850s, proposing that the rock was of extraterrestrial origins. It was long worshipped and revered by local people even before the development of Islam in the region. Muhammad himself was famously chosen to replace the sacred object following a ritual cleaning of the Kaaba. The rock was subsequently damaged during a siege of the city by the Umayyads in 683 and was stolen and ransomed by the Qarmatians during their rebellion in the tenth century. The Romans also acquired a number of sacred meteorites from their conquests, most notably the Needle of Cybele from Phrygia, which was carried back to Rome and worshipped for centuries. In the Americas, a number of tribes utilized, worshipped, and built settlements around numerous large meteorites. For example, the Clackamas tribe of Oregon traditionally dipped their arrowheads in water that pooled in the giant Willamette meteorite, feeling that it would give them greater accuracy and strength in battle.

As mentioned before, many premodern writers attempted to associate the arrivals of comets with the onset of epidemic disease as well. Thus in the first century AD, Marcus Manilius linked a comet to the outbreak of plague that crippled Athens and led to the death of Pericles. "Death comes with those celestial torches, which threaten earth with the blaze of pyres unceasing, since heaven and nature's self are stricken and seem doomed to share men's tomb." Later translator and poet in his own right, Alexander Pope, incorporated this still popular connection into his early eighteenth-century translation of the *Iliad*. Homer's original description of Achilles and his helmet shining like a star was recast with much political and astrological license into the following passage:

> Next, his high Head the Helmet grac'd; behind
> The sweepy Crest hung floating in the Wind:
> Like the red Star, that from his flaming Hair
> Shakes down Disease, Pestilence, and War.[19]

The ancients knew the gods and heaven to be fickle however. In 394 BC another comet blazed across the sky of Greece. Once again, this date is in keeping with a presumed appearance by Halley's Comet which most likely passed by Earth around 393–392 BC. With the fall of Athens, Sparta had become engaged with claiming various pieces of the Delian Empire. Predictably the various states of Greece joined with Persia to oppose these efforts, resulting in the Corinthian War of 395–387 BC. Around the time that Halley's Comet made its appearance the forces of Sparta engaged those of Athens and Persia at the Battle of Cnidus. The entire Spartan fleet was captured and destroyed and its commander killed. Any hope the Lacedaemonians had of constructing a Spartan trans-Aegean empire were destroyed. Conon went on to rebuild the Long Walls of Athens and Greece again split into warring factions. Pliny recorded the event:

> Other similar meteoric lights are "beams," in Greek *dokoi*, for example one that appeared when the Spartans were defeated at sea and lost the empire of Greece. There also occurs a yawning of the actual sky, called chasma, and also something that looks like blood, and a fire that falls from it to the earth—the most alarming possible cause of terror to mankind.[20]

Shortly afterward though, the main Spartan army under Agesilaus II, which was returning from Asia Minor, managed to defeat the other Greeks at Coronea and return to Sparta. Several other battles followed before peace was restored in 387 BC. Persia retained Ionia and Sparta was to remain the dominant Greek power in Hellas for a generation. The initial shock foretold by the comet was in this case short-lived.

Twenty-three years later, in 371 BC, another comet appeared and heralded in yet another defeat for Sparta. On July 6 of that year the reconstituted Boeotian League under Epaminondas dealt a devastating blow to the storied Spartan phalanx, using superior tactics to compensate for weaker warriors. Sparta's loss finally ended its dominance, which had existed in Hellas since the end of the Peloponnesian War and created a power vacuum that was soon to see the rise of Macedon to hegemony in the region. A similar event is described in 344 BC when a comet accompanied Timoleon's invasion of Sicily and the subsequent defeat of Syracuse. Diodorus of Sicily described it as "the gods foretold success by an extraordinary prodigy; A burning torch appeared in the Heavens for an entire night and went before the fleet into Sicily." Several other sources also reported long-lasting comets either at the Battle of Chaeronea in 338 BC, in which Philip of Macedon defeated the Greeks, or following his assassination and the rise to power of Alexander the Great three years later. Many of these stories were clearly later additions hoping to build on the prevailing fear and admiration for comets in Western society.

Roman sources overemphasized the appearance of comets when it came to their early rival for dominion in the western Mediterranean: Carthage. Interestingly, one of these involved the first verified sighting of Halley's Comet in the West. In May of 240 BC the great comet blazed its away across the sky of North Africa. At that time, Hamilcar Barca was bloodily putting down a mercenary revolt after the city's failure in the First Punic War. According to some later traditions, Hamilcar made his young son Hannibal swear under the light of the comet eternal animosity toward Rome. Interestingly, the family's surname, Barca, comes from the Semitic word for lightning, another ancient portent. Livy, however, assigns Hannibal's oath event to the latter's ninth year, placing it around 238 BC.[21] A similar event involving a different comet was described twenty years later as Hannibal prepared to launch the Second Punic War against Rome. As the Carthaginian's success waned and Scipio invaded North Africa, another comet or meteor appeared in Rome. Finally, Livy recorded a terrible comet seen in Asia Minor around 184 BC, the same year that Hannibal was hunted down and killed in the area. As an epilogue, comets were also reported to have appeared in 150 BC at the outbreak of the Third Punic War and in 146 BC when the city of Carthage itself was destroyed.

Thirteen years after Hannibal's initial descent into Italy, despite his failures to actually take the city of Rome, the inhabitants of the Republic were justifiably still fearful for the future and consulted various religious oracles. The augurs predicted that if the Idaean mother was brought from Pessinos to Rome, the enemy would be defeated.[22] This cryptic reference to the eastern cult of Cybele led the Romans to send a team of ambassadors toward the allied kingdom of Pergamum. "He then handed over to them the sacred stone which the natives declared to be 'the Mother of the Gods,' and bade them carry it to Rome."[23] After a harrowing voyage, the delegation returned with the meteorite to Rome and ceremoniously installed it in a temple. Many undoubtedly connected the acquisition of this otherworldly rock with the subsequent defeat of Hannibal only a few years later.

Roman historians repeated this storyline with the Republic's next great enemy, Mithridates of Pontus. Observers associated comets with his birth in 134 BC, his ascension to the throne in 119 BC, before his massacre of the Roman population of Asia Minor in 87 BC, and at his death in 63 BC.[24] While some of these may be doubtful, it is taken as fact that the astronomical phenomenon of 87 BC was a visit by Halley's Comet.

Perhaps one of the most successful uses of a comet for militaristic propaganda purposes came about as part of Octavian Augustus's attempts to legitimize his position during the civil wars of 44–30 BC. Around the beginning of the new millennium, Ovid penned the following regarding Julius Caesar, "Caesar is a god in his own city . . . a fiery comet."[25] The poet went on to describe how following his death, sounds of battle were heard in the sky and "firebrands were seen, burning in the midst of the stars."[26] Caesar's star, as it became known, was largely a later poetic attempt by the Romans to deify Augustus and his actions more than those of Caesar.[27] In fact, additional sightings of comets became retroactively associated with Caesar's birth, the rise of the First Triumvirate, and the beginning of his war with Pompey, which Cassius Dio recorded centuries later as, "fire which darted from

east to west," around 49 BC.[28] Though once again many of these cannot be substantiated, it is known that Halley's did revisit Earth in 87
BC ushering in Sulla's conquests in the east that led directly to Caesar's rise to power a generation later. In the years that followed the
fall of Caesar and the outbreak of civil war in Rome, Pliny recorded
the appearance of a comet, "that appeared at the time of the disaster
at Modena," where Decimus Brutus was besieged by Mark Antony in
44 BC.[29] A century later in AD 66, the historian Josephus recorded the
appearance of Halley's Comet, "a comet, that continued a whole year,"
as appearing before the outbreak of the Jewish rebellion that led to
the destruction of that city by Titus Flavius.[30] It is also important to
note that to the ancients, the region that a comet appeared from and
the direction in which it traveled were also of symbolic importance.
Thus the mention by Cassius Dio of a comet traveling from east to west
would have been used to show the shift in power and fortune between
Pompey in the east and Augustus in the west.

Even with the advent of Christianity, the idea that comets were
terrible portents of war and famine continued for over a thousand
years. Constantine's vision of a cross before the Battle of the Milvian
Bridge could have been caused by a meteorite, parhelion, or comet. As
recounted later by the emperor to Eusebius, "about noon, when the
day was already beginning to decline, he saw with his own eyes the tro-
phy of a cross of light in the heavens, above the Sun, and bearing the
inscription, Conquer by this. At this sight he himself was struck with
amazement, and his whole army also, which followed him on this expedition, and witnessed the miracle."[31] Tradition holds that the Roman
soldiers under his command then painted the symbol XP, for Christ,
on their shields and thereafter defeated the army of Maxentius.[32]

A number of such heavenly visitors are recorded at various points
during the collapse of Roman imperial rule. These include one in 399
AD which accompanied the invasion of Asia Minor by Tribigild, at Stili-
cho's defeat of the Goths in 405 AD, a cross-shaped comet that witnessed Alaric's sack of Rome in 410 AD, the return of Halley's Comet

in June of 451 AD in the same week that Attila the Hun's forces were decimated by a Roman, Gothic, and Frankish army at the Battle of the Catalaunian Plains, and finally at various points in the sixth century Goths and Germans ran rampant throughout Europe. Likewise, the fall of the Han Empire in China was also accompanied by the arrival of comets and meteors. In one of the most direct references to the effects of a comet on battle, Chinese historians record the appearance of just such an event in AD 185 as being the only reason that a group of well-armed and previously successful rebels stopped their advance on the imperial capital.[33]

One of the most well-documented appearances of Halley's Comet in premodern times occurred in March of 1066. Only two months after Harold was enthroned in England, Halley's Comet blazed across the skies, terrifying his vassals and citizens. As described by Theodricus Monachus in *De antiquitate regum Norwagiensium*, "For several days a comet appeared with a glowing red tail; and this prefigured the defeat of the English, which followed immediately afterwards."[34] Duke William of Normandy would employ the appearance of the comet as propaganda to discredit his rival, including a depiction of it in one of the opening scenes of the Bayeux Tapestry. Several months later his army landed in southeastern England and subsequently defeated Harold's at the Battle of Hastings. The Bayeux Tapestry remains perhaps the earliest pictorial representation of Halley's that survives to the present day.

Medieval European and Chinese historians recorded similar astral phenomena that occurred during the life of Tamerlane. Conquering vast swaths of Central and Southwest Asia, Tamerlane was viewed by contemporaries in much the same light as Mithridates and Hannibal. Three particular comets or meteors associated with him appeared in 1382, 1402, and 1405. The first saw the advent of his wars of conquest, the second the Battle of Ankara, and the third his death. Tamerlane actually used the comet of 1402, which moved from west to east across the sky, to bolster the fighting spirit of his men, predicting a great victory over the Ottomans should they attack. This is in keeping with Cassius Dio's interpretation of the east-to-west comet that appeared during the civil war following the assassination of Caesar. Tamerlane's subsequent victory at Ankara substantially weakened the Turkish empire, leading to a decade-long civil war that only his untimely death kept him from exploiting.

The fall of Constantinople in 1453, though not unforeseen, was still certainly viewed disastrously for the Western world. Despite calls by Popes Nicholas V and Calixtus III for the launching of a crusade against the Turks, little response came from Christendom. Meanwhile, Sultan Mehmed II continued to advance through southeastern Europe. As a lunar eclipse had accompanied the fall of Constantinople, eyes were undoubtedly focused on the night sky for any additional astral clues. As June of 1456 began, Halley's Comet suddenly made an appearance across central Europe. Twenty years later Bartolomeo Platina in his Papal history recorded the appearance of the comet and Calixtus's response.

> A hairy and reddish comet appearing for several days; as the mathematicians predicted an enormous pest, a drought, some great calamity: Calixtus in order to avert the wrath of God, ordered processions to be held on certain days: in order that if any evils were impending, He would turn them wholly on the Turks.

Later fallacious legends even held that the Pope was driven to excommunicate the comet in order to allay the fears of the peasants. Shortly after the comet left the skies, the Turks launched their attack on Belgrade, a siege that was to last until July 22. The great victory of Christendom was to preserve the area until 1521, ironically only a few years before another appearance of Halley's.

Emperor Maximilian proclaimed a meteorite that fell at Ensisheim, Germany in 1492 to be a good omen for his wars against the French and Turks. In a similar vein, a blood-red comet appeared in 1618 over Germany, heralding in the disastrous Thirty Years' War. So influential was the event that a children's rhyme arose from it, ever immortalizing not only the comet but fears of the phenomenon as well.

> Eight things a comet always brings,
> Wind, Famine, Plague, and Death to Kings,
> War, Earthquake, Floods, and Dire Things.

The almost constant wars of the next two hundred years meant that the appearance of almost every comet can be connected in some way with a battle or conflict. In 1759 alone during the return of Halley's Comet, a number of momentous engagements took place both in Europe and in America during the Seven Years' War. Yet by this point few in Europe or America would have placed much emphasis on a connection between the events.

Perhaps the last great man of history to have a comet associated with his rise and fall was Napoleon Bonaparte. In August of 1769, Charles Messier observed a large comet that would eventually blaze across the sky for over a month. Though unknown at the time, born during the appearance of the "broom star" was Napoleon, a man who was to blaze his own path across Europe. Several more heavenly manifestations occurred during his rise to power, with the most famous being the Great Comet of 1811. For almost nine months a large comet hurtled across Europe, eastward from France, before being last seen in the Russian sky. Its termination was almost immediately followed by Napoleon's ill-fated invasion of Russia, which some certainly saw as a terrestrial repetition of the celestial event of a year before. Much like Caesar before him, the former French emperor's death was accompanied by a comet, which was said to have appeared over France at the time of his demise in 1821.

America was not exempt from this concern over the appearance of meteors and comets. From May to August of 1861, a bright comet streaked across the Northern Hemisphere, reaching its height in July just as the First Battle of Bull Run was breaking out. A soldier recorded at the time that, "We have been visited for a week past by a very large comet which at full day appears very bright and transparent; late at night the tail stretched nearly to the Zenith while the star was near the horizon." In July of the next year, another great comet visited the night sky. Eventually christened the Swift-Tuttle Comet, its appearance during the Seven Days Battles heralded in the death and destruction that would see the halting of McClellan's attempts to take Richmond.

Overall, human history has been interspersed with the arrival of comets, meteors, and other heavenly visitors for thousands of years. While comets may have had no actual physical impact on the battlefield, the fear they engendered had a certain psychological effect. Likewise, they became useful explanations for why a battle was lost or as a piece of propaganda to promote a leader or general. Clearly, the impact of comets came largely from their unpredictable nature. Even when Halley finally identified his comet and predicted its return, it bore little relevance to the thousands of others that could visit the planet or perhaps even impact it. The recent hypothesis that a vast comet impact created the Cretaceous-Paleogene extinction has perhaps only increased our dread of the objects, reversing several centuries of scientific acceptance as harmless nighttime visitors. In 2013, the United Nations announced a plan for a worldwide effort to identify asteroids and comets that could potentially impact the planet, causing death and devastation.

Finally, the above-mentioned historical concerns may have in part inspired components of President Reagan's Strategic Defense Initiative (SDI), launched in 1983. "Star Wars," as it was derided in some media outlets, called for a collection of weapons platforms to both defend against nuclear attack and to deliver an offensive blow against the USSR. One of the more familiar components involved the development of kinetic weapons, nonexplosive objects that could be dropped from low orbit, accelerating to such a point that they would build up enough potential energy to make them capable of explosive power upon hitting the Earth. Known as Brilliant Pebbles, the weapons system became the centerpiece of the program before it was finally dismantled in the 1990s. The idea of harnessing the terrifying power of space in general and of falling objects specifically, marks a turning point in man's millennia-old struggle to interpret heavenly visitors.

2

ECLIPSES, THE SUN, AND THE MOON

To morrow, I believe, is to be an eclipse of the sun, and I think it perfectly meet and proper that the sun in the heavens, and the glory of the Republic should both go into obscurity and darkness together.
—BENJAMIN F. WADE, 1854

HEAVEN CONTAINS MUCH MORE THAN SIMPLY comets and asteroids. The motions and appearance of the planets, and especially their disappearance, were carefully tracked by almost all civilizations from the most primitive to the most advanced. Once again, early civilizations placed value on predictability and sought to use their observations to both calculate time and seasons as well as identify the will of the gods. Thus interpreters saw any minor deviation from a predicted path or an eclipse of the sun or moon as a negative omen.

ECLIPSES

When Benjamin Wade, a Radical Republican United States Senator, wrote the above line at the end of March in 1854, the nation was on the verge of being plunged into total civil war. The Kansas-Nebraska Act was passing through the Senate, leading to the collapse of the Whigs and the subsequent rise of the antislavery Republicans. As with comets and meteors, eclipses of either the sun or moon were viewed throughout history with fear and apprehension. In many ways they were seen as a far more terrible portent due to a number of factors. Foremost among these would have certainly been the fact that the daytime nature of solar eclipses would have made them visible to larger segments of the population. In addition, whether comets and meteors were falling stars, rocks thrown up by winds, or traveling bodies, their mechanics could at least be partially understood by most societies throughout history. Especially for early farming societies, the disappearance of the sun was a terrifying event. For many early societies the arrival of an eclipse announced not only astral imbalance but political imbalance as well. For countries built around the concept of the Mandate of Heaven or who saw the ruler as the chief priest who was responsible for keeping the seasons and astral cycles in balance, the occurrence meant a failure in leadership and the loss of rule.

One of the earliest written accounts of an eclipse occurred during the reign of King Mursili II of the Hittite Empire. Around 1312 BC, while he and his men were on campaign, a total eclipse was recorded as being visible. Despite its dramatic appearance though, no positive or negative effect is preserved in the literature of the time. One of the earliest recorded connections between an eclipse and the outbreak of actual revolutionary violence came in 763 BC. In June of that year, a near-total solar eclipse occurred in the Assyrian Empire. Ancient chronicles recorded the event and in the same line mentioned a rebellion in Assur, the old capital of the empire. Assyria had only just recovered from an outbreak of plague and the eclipse was simply a further sign that Ashur-dan III was unfit to rule. Though it appears the rebellion was short-lived, the nation remained in turmoil and almost constant strife until Tiglath-Pileser III seized power in 745 BC and restored order and prosperity. One of the more interesting tales of an eclipse occurred two centuries later in late May of 585 BC. According to Herodotus:

> Afterwards, on the refusal of Alyattes to give up his suppliants when Cyaxares sent to demand them of him, war broke out between the Lydians and the Medes, and continued for five years, with various success. In the course of it the Medes gained many victories over the Lydians, and the Lydians also gained many victories over the Medes. Among their other battles there was one night engagement. As, however, the balance had not inclined in favor of either nation, another combat took place in the sixth year, in the course of which, just as the battle was growing warm, day was on a sudden changed into night. This event had been foretold by Thales, the Milesian, who forewarned the Ionians of it, fixing for it the very year in which it actually took place. The Medes and Lydians, when they observed the change, ceased fighting, and were alike anxious to have terms of peace agreed on.[35]

Whether both sides took the event as a message from the gods or the Medes were overawed by the power of the Lydians to predict the event, the eclipse of 585 BC brought an end to the Battle of the Halys and preserved the small kingdom of Lydia for another thirty-nine years until it was finally reduced by Cyrus the Great. Obviously it is just as likely that the battle was halted for other reasons or simply that the Lydians won outright.

Herodotus recorded a number of pivotal eclipses during the Persian Wars. The first occurred as the massive Persian army was gathering at Sardis before crossing over to Europe.

> After they had passed the winter at Sardis, the army set forth from thence fully equipped, at the beginning of spring, to march to Abydos; and when it had just set forth, the Sun left his place in the heaven and was invisible, though there was no gathering of clouds and the sky was perfectly clear; and instead of day it became night. When

Xerxes saw and perceived this, it became a matter of concern to him; and he asked the Magians what the appearance meant to portend. These declared that the god was foreshowing to the Hellenes a leaving of their cities, saying that the Sun was the foreshower of events for the Hellenes, but the Moon for the Persians. Having been thus informed, Xerxes proceeded on the march with very great joy.[36]

While the date and even the existence of this eclipse is much in question, its component as a matter of divination to predict the outcome of the war would have certainly occurred either with this event or some other natural occurrence.[37] Not all of the Persian allies were comforted by the announcements of the magi though. According to Herodotus, Pythius, a descendant of the last king of Lydia and now a nominal ally of Xerxes, took fright at the eclipse and asked that one of his five sons be released from the army. Perhaps worried that doing so would spread fear among his ranks, the emperor instead "commanded those to whom it was appointed to do these things, to find out the eldest of the sons of Pythius and to cut him in two in the middle; and having cut him in two, to dispose the halves, one on the right hand of the road and the other on the left, and that the army should pass between them by this way."[38]

The magi seem to have been at least partially correct as the unprecedented Persian army crossed into Europe and subdued all before them. Following the disaster at Thermopylae, the Greeks fell back to the Isthmus of Corinth, hoping to make a stand there behind a well-constructed wall. As the various Hellenic allies were busily finishing up defensive preparations, a second eclipse allegedly appeared in the sky in October of 480 BC. The leader of the Spartans and their tributary states was the regent Cleombrotus, the brother of the slain Leonidas. Herodotus recorded that, "whilst he was offering sacrifice to know if he should march out against the Persians, the sun was suddenly darkened in mid sky." Apparently Cleombrotus saw the omen as a negative one and instantly withdrew himself back to Sparta. He died soon after returning, with some attributing his early demise to the eclipse itself. Regardless, he was now replaced in command by Pausanias, whose acumen went on to defeat the Persians at Platea and drive them fully from Greece.

The massive Peloponnesian War that followed the expulsion of Persia from the Aegean contained an incident that revolved around yet another eclipse. In August of 413 BC, after having failed to achieve success in their Sicilian Expedition, the Athenian military commanders had decided to withdraw back to Greece. According to Thucydides:

> The preparations were made and they were on the point of sailing, when the moon, being just then at the full, was eclipsed. The mass of the army was greatly moved, and called upon the generals to remain. Nicias himself, who was too much under the influence of divination and such like, refused even to discuss the question of their removal until they had remained thrice nine days, as the soothsayers prescribed. This was the reason why the departure of the Athenians was finally delayed.[39]

Nicias's hesitation due to the eclipse proved to be costly as the Syracusans took the opportunity to launch a coordinated assault on the Athenian navy. The majority of the Greek fleet was either destroyed or forced onto the beaches.

A month-long Sicilian siege of the Athenian camp followed during which disease, heat, thirst, and starvation crippled the Greek army. Finally, Nicias and the other commanders attempted to break out of the encirclement, only to be surrounded and massacred at the Assinarus River. Most of the Athenians were either killed or sold into slavery, including Nicias and Demosthenes who were both executed. The Sicilian eclipse of 413 BC had cost the Athenians their chance of continuing the war much longer. News of the defeat led to the downfall of the Athenian government as well and ushered in the loss of the Peloponnesian War several years later.

A century later the resurgent Greek world under Alexander the Great was marching across the Near East seeking to finally defeat the Persian Empire. Eleven days before his final victory at Gaugamela in October of 331 BC, the slowly approaching armies experienced a lunar eclipse. As retold by Plutarch, "There happened an eclipse of the Moon, about the beginning of the festival of the great mysteries at Athens. The eleventh night after that eclipse, the two armies being in view of each other, Darius kept his men under arms, and took a general review of his troops by torch-light."[40] Alexander's generals offered sacrifices and determined the event to be a positive sign for the Greeks. Apparently the Persians took an opposite view as many of the Macedonian generals urged their king to launch a sudden attack on the enemy at night. Alexander famously quipped that, "I will not steal a victory," and instead launched his carefully planned attack days later.

A similar story unfolded a century and a half later at Pydna in 168 BC. The Third Macedonian War had been raging for over three years as Lucius Aemilius Paulus descended upon the army of King Perseus. The night before battle was joined a lunar eclipse appeared over the region. The Macedonians apparently became frightened, seeing the sign as favoring Rome. Plutarch recorded:

> The Romans, according to their custom, clattering brass pans and lifting up fire-brands and torches into the air, invoked the return of her light; the Macedonians behaved far otherwise: Terror and amazement seized their whole army, and a rumor crept by degrees into their camp that this eclipse portended even that of their king. Aemilius was no novice in these things, nor was ignorant of the nature of the seeming irregularities of eclipses—that in a certain revolution of time, the moon in her course enters the shadow of the earth and is there obscured, till, passing the region of darkness, she is again enlightened by the sun. Yet being a devout man, a religious observer of sacrifices and the art of divination, as soon as he perceived the moon beginning to regain her former luster, he offered up to her eleven heifers.[41]

Paulus's men, well rested and unfazed by the eclipse, won a resounding victory the next day. Perseus was captured, Macedonia was devastated and divided, and Rome emerged as the dominant power in the Greek region.

As mentioned in the previous chapter, the Battle of the Milvian Bridge, which brought both Constantine and Christianity into power in the West, was influenced by a heavenly phenomenon. A strong possibility exists that the strange sighting in the sky was a sun dog or parhelion, an occurrence where multiple suns, often in the shape of a cross, appear on the horizon. This explanation seems to fit the evidence that exists in the historical record better than the appearance of a comet or other body.

Five hundred years later, a much more pious Catholic took the sight of an eclipse quite differently than Constantine, and in so doing brought about the gradual evolution of modern Europe. In May of 840, Louis the Pious, the only surviving son of Charlemagne, observed a total solar eclipse from his palace at Ingelheim. Later legends hold that the king was so frightened by this omen, following so closely upon his launching of a series of bloody wars, that the pious man died of fear only a few days later. Regardless of the cause, his death split the empire into civil war. The resulting Treaty of Verdun would permanently divide western Europe into what would emerge as France, Germany, and Italy, a division that doomed any hope of reuniting the old Western Roman Empire.

Eclipses also were seen as omens of disaster even when they did not directly occur around the time of battle or particular event. Some of the more famous include one in July of 523 BC which was followed by the death of Cambyses of Persia, another in 306 AD which witnessed the death of Constantine, an eclipse in 1009 directly preceding Caliph Mansur al-Hakim's destruction and desecration of Jerusalem, and the eclipse of May 1453 which many saw as fulfillment of an old prophecy that the fall of Constantinople was imminent.

A little over a thousand years after the Battle of the Milvian Bridge the appearance of another parhelion once again helped to promote victory in a battle. Having only just been named leader of the Yorkist cause following the death of his father in December of 1460, Edward of York advanced to the southwest to defeat a Lancastrian army gathering near the Welsh border. On the morning of February 2, 1461, the camp observed a parhelion. Edward saw the sign as the mark of either the Holy Trinity or him and his three brothers, rallied his men, and, "tooke suche courage, that he fiercely setting on his emimyes, put them to flight."[42] His success at the Battle of Mortimer's Cross began his slow but steady march to London and his subsequent coronation as King Edward IV. To commemorate the battle, Edward later adopted the sun as his personal badge, demonstrating his belief that it played a central role, if not in the battle, then at least in the propaganda of the event.

The impact of solar and lunar phenomena on war declined markedly with the birth of modern astronomy and the Scientific Revolution. Yet, the growth of conflicts between Western forces and more superstitious native tribes and kingdoms in the nineteenth century meant that once again eclipses would not only matter in conflict, but could be used by the more modernized West against its more primitive opponents.

One of the greatest examples of this remains the conquest of the Aztec Empire by the Spanish between 1519 and 1521. Native writings and later tales list a number of natural phenomena that are said to have presaged the arrival of European armies in Mexico. Included among these were a rain of fire that fell upon the capital city, a lightning strike on the temple of Xiuhtecuhtli, comets, and floods. Much like the natural disasters that drove the Mandate of Heaven in Chinese political history, these events were later interpreted as forewarnings of the disaster that followed.

Following the American Revolution, the new nation that emerged from the Thirteen Colonies found one of its most pressing problems to be the innumerous bands of Native Americans that lay just beyond the Pennsylvania frontier. The previous century of American expansion had taught the Indians that the progress of Europeans westward was largely inevitable and unavoidable. By far the most successful attempt at resisting this juggernaut was the coalition pieced together by King Philip in the 1670s to resist the growth of the Puritan colonies in New England. Though in the end the English were victorious, their triumph came at a loss of 5–8 percent of the male population of New England, a casualty rating higher than that of Germany, the United Kingdom, or the United States in World War II.

The Shawnee brothers Tecumseh and the Prophet took this lesson to heart and sought to organize an even larger such coalition in the Ohio region. Yet to unite such disparate groups required more than just ideas and ambition. The Prophet billed himself as a religious leader who sought to expel the Americans through the power of the Great Spirit. A number of factors aided in his rise to power including the outbreak of disease among the tribes, further encroachments by white settlers, and most notably an eclipse in 1806. Gathering a number of influential leaders around him, the Prophet had predicted the onset of a solar eclipse in June of 1806, convincing many of the Indians of the region of his spiritual powers. However, despite what his followers thought, the Prophet's abilities of prognostication were completely fabricated. Tecumseh and his brother had learned of the impending eclipse from some traveling Americans, utilizing the very science of the white man they were seeking to drive out and replace with more traditional values. Ironically, it is recorded that William Henry Harrison, then governor of Indiana Territory, had actually been the one to challenge the various tribes in his area to test the prophetical ability of the Prophet and Tecumseh, a test that would spell trouble for him in the future.

Five years later, as Napoleon's Comet was blazing across Europe, Tecumseh allegedly predicted yet another solar eclipse, this one was accompanied by the massive New Madrid Earthquake of 1811. The Indian chief's foreknowledge of both served to further polarize the region. In response, Governor Harrison moved toward Prophetstown resulting in a fierce fight with the confederacy at Tippecanoe. The subsequent defeat of the Natives and their retreat into Canada served as an impetus for the War of 1812.

Nor were the Shawnee brothers the first inhabitants of the New World to utilize the movements of the Sun to cement their place in power. At some point prior to the arrival of the Europeans, the various Iroquoian-speaking tribes of upper New York united into a confederation that would make them one the most powerful force in the northeast for centuries. According to oral tales, the different tribes had spent years fighting each other to no avail. A prophet of peace arose named Deganawida who began to unite the clans beginning with the Mohawk to the east. The last nation to submit, the Seneca, did so after a dramatic solar eclipse, which they interpreted as demonstrating the power of the Great Peacemaker. "A moan of terrible fear went up from the warriors—men who could meet death on the chase or in the battle with a smile were unnerved by that awful spectacle. They saw a black disc moving forward over the face of an unclouded sun."[43] Awed into submission the final Indians joined what would be the only democracy in the western hemisphere and one of the strongest powers to confront the Europeans and Americans. Interestingly, many historians have attempted to utilize the eclipse itself to date the event. While arguments have been made for years that the confederation was formed in either the fifteenth or sixteenth centuries, the nearest total solar eclipse in the region occurred in 1142, pushing back the date of the formation of the confederacy by over three hundred years.[44]

Christopher Columbus would experience two eclipses while exploring the New World. The first of these was in 1494 near Hispaniola, while the second occurred a decade later. During the latter event, Columbus and his crew were stranded on the island of Jamaica. With their ships damaged and beached, the Italian explorer and his crew were only able to survive thanks to the hospitality of the local tribe. Yet after six months, the Taino halted trading with the Europeans and the Spaniards faced a dire future. According to an account delivered by his son years later, Columbus consulted his copy of a famed astronomical work and determined that a lunar eclipse would soon be visible over the island. The explorer used this knowledge to spread fear among the Taino and ensure the survival of his men. "With great howling and lamentation they came running from every direction to the ships, laden with provisions, praying the Admiral to intercede by all means with God on their behalf; that he might not visit his wrath upon them."[45]

The effect of eclipses on Native Americans continued well into the nineteenth century. In August of 1869, George Davidson trekked into the Chilkat Valley along the Alaskan Panhandle to observe an eclipse of the sun. Recent, violent engagements between settlers in the region and the local natives had left tensions high and Davidson had been warned to expect possible attack. Upon encountering the local tribe, the explorer explained that his mission was purely scientific and predicted the upcoming eclipse. When the event occurred, the Indians, either terrified or content to accept his reason for being in their territory, quickly disappeared into the woods. Davidson's knowledge of the impending event helped to prevent bloodshed and saved his party.

Yet even for these native people the danger associated with eclipses of either the sun or moon was eventually to wane. By the end of the nineteenth century even the most distant population saw the event as little more than a novelty or distraction. During the Battle of Isandl-wana in January of 1879, a brief total solar eclipse did little more than momentarily distract from the slaughter taking place on the field. As one warrior recounted, "The sun turned black in the middle of the battle; we could still see it over us, or should have thought we had been fighting till evening. Then we got into the camp, and there was a great deal of smoke and firing. Afterwards the sun came out bright again."[46]

World War I as a conflict straddled the Romantic and Modern Ages. As such, apart from the advances in technology and tactics, much of the classical beliefs in gentleman's warfare and soldiers' superstitions were still present. Not surprisingly then, much hay was made of the total eclipse that blanketed parts of Europe in August of 1914 just as the war was unfolding and the Germans were pushing their way across Belgium. The London based *Star* periodical published a cartoon for the event showing the shadow of the Kaiser obscuring the bright surface of the sun in a not so subtle reference to the battle as one of the forces of light against those of darkness.[47]

The vast and total destruction caused by the war weighed heavily on the hearts and minds of Europeans at the time. This perhaps helps to explain in part the great miracle that occurred at Fatima in Portugal in October of 1917, a year before the end of the conflict. Three young children experienced numerous apparitions of the Virgin Mary during the summer and fall of that year. In July of 1917 during one of the appearances, the children reported that Mary promised an end to World War I and that a sign would follow to prove this at her last visit. True to form on October 13 as tens of thousands gathered at Fatima, many reported what became known as the Miracle of the Sun as the orb appeared to change color or dance through the sky. While various commentators have either dismissed the claim or else argued for a parhelion, the message to believers was clear, the war would soon end, and as revealed in the Second Secret of Fatima, a far greater one would soon start. Indeed, on January 25, 1938, a rare occurrence of the aurora borealis occurred as far south as North Africa. The next month Hitler moved into Austria and shortly afterward Czechoslovakia. Many Roman Catholics saw this as clear confirmation of what was revealed at Fatima a generation before.

While both worship for and fear of the sun have died out around most of the world, its ability to cause actual destruction has only increased with the growth of modern technology. Solar storms, the expulsion of large waves of charged particles from the sun, occur periodically but were not first observed and recorded until 1859. In early September of that year several scientists noticed solar flares emerging from the sun and telegraph systems around the Northern Hemisphere began to fail or even electrocute their operators. A newspaper of the day reported that, "The auroral display of last night was so brilliant after midnight that ordinary print could be read by its light.

It considerably impeded the working of the telegraph lines."[48] The increased reliance upon electrical power and circuits by both civilians and the military in the twentieth century merely increased the potential damage that could be caused by a large enough solar storm. In 1989 an Australian army unit arrived in Namibia as part of a peacekeeping operation at the same time that a massive coronal ejection erupted from the sun's corona. High-frequency radios used by the Australians were knocked out for days or longer resulting in a near complete lack of communication.

Perhaps the closest any nation has come to disaster due to solar activity occurred in 1967. In late May of that year, a key component of America's defensive system against Soviet attack, the Ballistic Missile Early Warning System in the Arctic, suddenly went down at three locations. The Air Force readied nuclear laden planes, not sure if this was a Russian attempt at jamming in preparation for an all-out launch or whether it was a naturally occurring event that would blind them to a Soviet attack. The US Solar Forecasting had been observing the phenomenon and NORAD eventually notified its bases and commanders of the effects that the solar flare might have. The news came just as the Air Force was set to respond. Nuclear war was averted thanks to the military's decision years earlier to invest in the study of space weather and phenomena.[49] While no major solar storm has coincided with a battle or war, the potential exists and will only increase in the future as militaries become more reliant on satellites and drones.

THE MOON AND DARKNESS

Even when it was not mysteriously disappearing or changing colors, the moon has always played a role in human society just as it has in the systematic progressions of nature. Perhaps its greatest impact has been as a purveyor of fear. The night was always a time of fear and terror for early man, due in part to his diurnal nature, limited night vision, and the abundance of nocturnal predators. Natural, physical limitations combined with organizational challenges to restrict coordinated, large-scale military actions being undertaken at night. In fact, while history is replete with night raids, few if any large-scale combat took place during the hours of darkness before the latter twentieth century. Yet, certain commanders in history have appreciated and utilized the value of darkness during their campaigns, often changing the course of history by doing so.

The Bible contains one of the earliest references to night combat, though as more of an allusion or miracle. Both 2 Kings and 2 Chronicles describe the eighth-century BC attack by Sennacherib upon Jerusalem following King Hezekiah's revolt. After a lengthy siege, the Jews seemed to be on the verge of defeat. "That night the angel of the Lord went out and put to death a hundred and eighty-five thousand in the Assyrian camp. When the people got up the next morning—there were all the dead bodies! So Sennacherib king of Assyria broke camp and withdrew. He returned to Nineveh and stayed there."[50] It seems that Hezekiah's policy of depriving the enemy of water led to the outbreak of endemic disease among the besiegers. Whether or not the reference to an angel of the Lord, or the Angel of Death as recorded by Lord Byron, alluded to simply disease or perhaps continued, periodic night raids on the enemy camp, the idea of a nocturnal destruction of the enemy was seen as a powerful victory. In fact, historian William H. McNeill posited that this night victory helped to preserve the religion, cement monotheism in Israel, and eventually led to the subsequent rise of both Christianity and Islam.[51]

The Ionian Revolt and subsequent Persian Wars provide us with the first verifiable night actions in combat. In 496 BC, the Carians managed to surprise and decimate a Persian force during a night ambush at Pedasus, helping to delay the conquest of the region. Likewise, the first attempt by Darius to punish the Greeks for aiding the Ionians was stopped on land by a Macedonian night assault in 492 BC. Clearly this was being chosen as a tactic by inferior forces in order to compensate for smaller numbers. Perhaps it is not surprising that the Spartans at the Battle of Thermopylae, outnumbered and doomed, would again think to utilize the darkness of night as a force multiplier. Several ancient historians wrote that during the several day-long Persian assaults on the mountain pass, the Spartans undertook a nighttime raid of the enemy camp. Having been told by an oracle that either the king of Persia or the city of Sparta would fall, Leonidas and his men decided to pursue the former.

> They immediately seized their arms, and six hundred men rushed into the camp of five hundred thousand, making directly for the king's tent, and resolving either to die with him, or, if they should be overpowered, at least in his quarters. An alarm spread through the whole Persian army. The Spartans being unable to find the king, marched uncontrolled through the whole camp, killing and overthrowing all that stood in their way, like men who knew that they fought, not with the hope of victory, but to avenge their own deaths. The contest was protracted from the beginning of the night through the greater part of the following day. At last, not conquered, but exhausted with conquering, they fell amidst vast heaps of slaughtered enemies.[52]

Though Herodotus does not mention the assault numerous other sources do, presenting it as a final climatic assault by the trapped Spartans. For his part, Herodotus employs night to cover the Persian's own assault on the Spartan position. The Greek traitor Ephialtes, after informing Xerxes of the small path that led around the defenders' position, took the Persians on a night march in order to envelop the Greeks in the morning. Regardless of which side utilized the cover of darkness, it had clearly become a viable option for large armies. Alexander the Great undertook just such a night maneuver in May of 326 BC prior to crossing Hydaspes River in India and defeating King Porus. Likewise, the Roman general Regulus used darkness to position his troops in order to effectively defeat the Carthaginians at the Battle of Adys in 255 BC and Cleomenes III of Sparta utilized night marches to hold off Macedonian attacks for years and to capture the impregnable city of Argos.

Yet, that is not to suggest that nocturnal operations had become perfected. For example, Pausanias's nighttime retreat from the field at Plataea proved to be so disorganized that it resulted in the final great battle with Persian forces on Greek soil the next morning. Only the superior equipment and battle acumen of the Spartans managed to prevent the utter defeat that should have resulted from the botched march. A century later in 390 BC, a Gallic tribe, the Senones, went to war with the Roman Republic after the latter had violated ambassadorial neutrality. Following the utter defeat of the Roman army at the Battle of the Allia River, the Gauls, under Brennus, entered the undefended capital and began to loot it. The remaining Romans had largely fled to the fortress atop the Capitoline Hill where they intended to wait out the barbarian raid. Unfortunately, the Gauls found a narrow path that the Romans were using to ascend to and descend from the fortress and therefore planned a subsequent night assault. According to Livy . . .

> Choosing a night when there was a faint glimmer of light, they sent an unarmed man in advance to try the road; then handing one another their arms where the path was difficult, and supporting each other or dragging each other up as the ground required, they finally reached the summit. So silent had their movements been that not only were they unnoticed by the sentinels, but they did not even wake the dogs, an animal peculiarly sensitive to nocturnal sounds. But they did not escape the notice of the geese, which were sacred to Juno and had been left untouched in spite of the extremely scanty supply of food. This proved the safety of the garrison, for their clamor and the noise of their wings aroused M. Manlius, the distinguished soldier, who had been consul three years before.[53]

Manlius led a counterassault, which pushed back the attackers and saved the fortress. An outbreak of disease further enervated the Gallic will to fight and both sides soon reached a peace accord. The timely return of Camillus with an army then provided for the ultimate doom of Brennus's invasion.

A century later, in 251 BC, a young exile of Sicyon carried out a much more successful night assault. After over a decade of tyrannical rule, Aratus, the son of a previous magistrate returned with a small team of exiles and scaled the unguarded city walls under cover of darkness. Having captured the guards, Aratus was able to rally the population to his cause. By the end of the day the tyrant Nicocles had fled and the city was once again free. Night usually favored the movement of smaller units over larger armies. This was proven again in the year 1102 when King Baldwin of Jerusalem was able to extricate himself from the fortress at Ramlah where he was besieged by an Egyptian army. Traveling to Arsuf, Baldwin was quickly able to raise a small force and subsequently defeat the enemy at Jaffa.

It seems that occasionally night attacks were utilized to help spread fear among the enemy. This was especially true when fire was employed as a weapon at the same time. During the Siege of Rhodes in 304 BC, both Demetrius Poliocretes of Macedonia and the Rhodians unleashed flaming arrows, burning firepots, and fire bolts loosed from ballistae to both injure and frighten the enemy. The historian Diodorus of Sicily wrote that "the fire missiles burned bright as they hurtled violently through the air."

The Roman dictator, L. Cornelius Sulla, employed a number of night attacks during his rise to power. In 82 BC as he engaged the forces of Gaius Marius the Younger in battle for the control of southern Italy, forces loyal to Sulla staged a successful night assault on Naples.[54] The city fell and along with it most of the Roman fleet. Shortly afterward Sulla himself heard of a Samnite army approaching Rome and therefore rushed to establish a camp outside of the Colline Gate. The Battle of the Colline Gate, though ultimately deciding the civil war, did not start out in Sulla's favor. Both sides advanced in late afternoon and though victorious on his right, Sulla's left was defeated and pushed back to the very threshold of the city gate itself. The action most likely would have ended here had not the defenders on the wall brought the gate crashing down, trapping Sulla's men outside of the city. With no alternative left, the men turned and reengaged the Samnites. According to Appian, "they fought all night and killed a great number."[55] Sulla was victorious in the end and secured himself as dictator of Rome. It is doubtful that the Samnites sought for a nighttime engagement. On the contrary, they most likely hoped that their late-afternoon attack would prevent the Romans from launching a counterattack should they be pushed back quickly enough toward the walls. The dogged determination of Sulla's men to once more engage the enemy, even though night had fallen, secured for him the republic.

Indeed, even for the great Roman military machine, night engagements were preserved for the direst of situations. Just over fifty years after the death of Julius Caesar, the Roman Empire suffered its first major defeat in the forest of western Germany. Publius Quinctilius Varus led three legions across the Rhine in an attempt to put down what he perceived to be a minor Germanic rebellion. Marching through the Teutoburg Forest, the loosely organized Romans were surrounded and ultimately massacred by tens of thousands of Germans. Only the failure of the Germans to continue the slaughter into the night, combined with the ability of the Romans to construct encampments in the dark, preserved Varus's army for another day of battle. Following a second slaughter the next day the Romans again encamped, but only as a temporary measure. As soon as the Germans had bedded down for the night, the legions attempted to escape from the area by a night march. Anticipating this, Arminius had surrounded the enemy's position with a defensive wall, thus penning the Romans in and assuring their subsequent destruction once the sun had risen.

During the Year of the Four Emperors, in AD 69, a situation similar to the Colline Gate incident reoccurred, after almost 150 years. As Vespasian gathered his strength in the east, a collection of legions along the Danube under Marcus Antonius Primus marched on Italy in the name of the former general. On the road to Cremona, Antonius

encountered an army loyal to Vespasian's rival, Vitellius. The Second
Battle of Bedriacum lasted through the night, proving costly for both
sides. As the sun rose, the III Gallica legion turned to the east to salute
it. Vitellius's men became convinced that reinforcements were arriving
and began to flee. Antonius burned Cremona to the ground, opening
the way to Rome for Vespasian.

Attila's march into Western Europe was conducted on a massive
scale that made the battlefield quite fluid and left much room for error.
While shadowing the invading force, a group of Roman-allied Franks
accidently encountered a band of Hunnic Gepids, slaughtering thousands in the dark. The main Roman and the Hunnic armies finally
collided at the Battle of the Catalaunian Plains in an engagement that
was seen as deciding the immediate future of the Roman world. It
appears that the Hunnic leader followed a similar tactic to the Samnites at the Colline Gate. Taking most of the day to organize his men,
Attila launched his attack in late afternoon, hoping that nightfall
would prevent a counterattack by the defeated enemy. Only the superior strength and speed of the Visigoths secured victory for Flavius
Aetius and the Romans, driving Attila back into his laagered camp as
night fell. Once again though, darkness brought chaos to both sides as
Thorismund, the new leader of the Franks, stumbled into the Hunnic
camp and Aetius himself became lost during the night. In this case
the onset of darkness saved Attila from utter destruction but could
not reverse the course of his defeat. The Western Roman Empire had
been saved from immediate destruction and conflagration and instead
became subjected to slow enervation.

Night attacks were not just rare in European military history, but
that of other nations and regions as well. One of the few exceptions
seems to have been in Japan during the Genpei War, which brought
about the rise of the Shogun. A number of battles, raids, and sieges
took place after the fall of darkness, some by design and some by accident. The first major action undertaken by the Minamoto clan against
their rival, the Taira, occurred in 1180 as they set out from Izu Province.

Oba Kagechika launched a night assault on the Minamoto camp at Ishibashiyama, effectively destroying much of the enemy's strength. Shortly afterward, the two sides again faced each other near Mount Fuji. A flock of waterfowl taking off at night were mistaken by the Taira forces for a surprise attack and they quickly fled in fear. The next year, further to the south, a Minamoto army under Minamoto Yukiie performed a night crossing of a small river near Sunomata to launch a surprise attack on the enemy. The Taira though, were expecting just such a move and after allowing the enemy to cross, launched an attack. The Taira soldiers allegedly solved the problem of identifying the enemy at night by attacking anyone who was wet.[56] Likewise, the turning point of the war came at the Battle of Kurikara, where Minamoto no Yoshinaka utilized a nighttime encirclement to surround and defeat the gathered Taira forces. Finally, the Battle of Yashima, which secured Shikoku for the Minamoto, also involved a night advance on the part of the latter army. The willingness of the Japanese to engage in more night actions and movement by night than other armies may lie in their lighter armor and lack of use of unified lines in combat and reliance instead upon individual combat. Thus unit cohesion was of less importance and this allowed for tactics that were unworkable in the rest of Europe and Asia.

As various Native American groups used similar small-scale tactics, night attacks and raids again became a phenomenon during the Spanish and English conquest of the New World. In the 1540s and 1550s during the Arauco War in Chile, for example, the native Mapuche people would attack the Spanish under Pedro de Valdivia at night on at least two occasions. The first of these occurred in 1546 at Quilacura while the second was in 1550 as the Spanish were camped at Andalien. In both instances the Indians attempted to use surprise to counter the technological and equine advantages of the invaders, but to no avail. Each battle saw the Mapuche lose thousands of men to only a handful of Spanish deaths. General Anthony Wayne's nighttime assault on Stony Point in 1779 can be seen as arising from a similar idea, negating the numerical, defensive, and firepower advantages of the British by assaulting the fortress at night.

Continuing the tactics of Alexander the Great, many generals and kings would use night as a convenient shield by which to position troops for early-morning attacks. Knights on the First Crusade utilized just such a maneuver twice in 1098 in order to both repel an attack by Turks and to take the heavily garrisoned city of Antioch. The increased usage of heavy armor and clanking artillery during the Renaissance would seem to have negated the idea of night marches. Yet, Spanish and Imperial troops under Charles de Lannoy used an artillery bombardment to shield a nocturnal march by his troops in order to better position himself for an assault on the French army at the Battle of Pavia in 1525. Centuries later the English would do the same at the climactic Battle of the Plains of Abraham, sailing their soldiers up the St. Lawrence during the night with muffled oars and marching up a side path to be ready to assault Quebec in the morning. Perhaps the most famous of these maneuvers occurred in 1776 when American soldiers under General Washington performed a night crossing of the Delaware in order to launch an early-morning assault on the Hessians at Trenton.

The massive Ottoman invasion of Europe must have reminded many at the time of the Persian rush into Europe 1800 years before. The majority of those that faced the Turks in open battle were crushed and their kingdoms incorporated into the growing empire. Vlad III Tepes, better known as Vlad the Impaler, and his small nation of Wallachia was the next target of Ottoman expansion following the fall of much of the Balkans. Outnumbered and unsupported, Vlad chose to rely on night as an ally to stop the Turkish advance. Having learned that the Sultan had ordered his men to remain in their tents that night, Vlad opted for a series of raids into the enemy camp once darkness had fallen. His tactic worked, and over the course of several hours Vlad "sped like lightning in every direction and caused great slaughter, so much so that, had the other commander to whom he had entrusted his remaining forces been equally brave, or had the Turks not fully obeyed the repeated orders from the sultan not to abandon their garrisons, the Wallachian undoubtedly would have gained the greatest and most brilliant victory."[57] When combined with his legendary impalement of twenty thousand Turks, Vlad convinced the sultan to return over the Danube, saving Wallachia and central Europe.

The Turks themselves had utilized a similar tactic in 1371 when they themselves faced a much larger opponent. In order to halt the Turkish invasion of the Balkans, the Serbian king Vukašin Mrnjavčević had gathered a massive army together and planned to make a sudden attack on the relatively unguarded Turkish capital of Edirne. In response a small Ottoman force of under a thousand men launched a night raid on the Serbian camp at Chernomen near the Maritsa. Thousands were killed, including King Vukašin, and the only substantial force between the Turks and the conquest of both Bulgaria and Serbia was decimated.

Yet, desperate night attacks were not always successful. The Duke of Monmouth's failed nocturnal assault upon the forces of King James II at Sedgemoor in 1685 represents one such blunder. In this case a lack of training, equipment, and cavalry meant that Monmouth's men were unable to deliver the decisive blow necessary upon surprising the enemy army. Likewise, sixty years later the Jacobites, under Bonnie Prince Charles Edward Stuart, attempted a failed night attack against Nairn. Once again a lack of coordination and communication in the dark ultimately doomed the expedition. The subsequent Battle of Culloden the next day ended the rebellion.

Night and naval warfare seems to have intersected even more frequently than in traditional combat. With the advent of the cannon as the main weapon in sea battles, the need to approach the enemy became less important than the need to disguise one's own position. Additionally, much of traditional naval warfare consisted of inadvertently encountering an enemy fleet, thus producing battles outside of the standard time frame for combat. Failure to engage the enemy when he is found, regardless of the time, could lead to losing the enemy should he choose to flee. Examples of this include Drake at Cadiz in

1587, Nelson at the Nile in 1798, and Saumarez at the Second Battle of Algeciras Bay in 1801. The famed Battle of Fort McHenry, which produced the *Star-Spangled Banner,* was also a night engagement, with the British lighting off Congreve rockets to coordinate their bombardment of the American bastion. This continued into the twentieth century as well with the greatest naval engagement of World War I, the Battle of Jutland, stretching from afternoon until after dark.

Perhaps the most famous planned nighttime naval engagements occurred at Calais in 1588. Finding the Spanish Armada docked there for the night, the English unleashed a wave of fireships, which broke up the Spanish formation and allowed for their subsequent defeat. Likewise, the war in the Pacific in the 1940s saw the frequent use of night attacks by Japanese ships and planes to counter American naval superiority. In late 1943 and early 1944 the uss *Enterprise* pioneered the use of night fighting and night bombing by an American carrier, a tactic that would come to serve her well in the waters off of the Philippines in 1945.

The horrors involved in the American Civil War and World War I and frequent stalemates reached on the battlefield prompted the investigation of night attacks as a plausible alternative. Some of this may have been inspired by the Duke of Wellington's successful night assault on the walled city of Badajoz in 1812. Yet, much of the impetus for the Duke's assault came from the fact that Marshal Soult was approaching to relieve the endangered bastion. In the end the tremendous casualties suffered by the English and Portuguese in taking the town resulted in a complete breakdown of discipline and an orgy of looting and violence for days. Despite the best attempts of later commanders to copy Wellington's success, once again issues of command and control served to hamper any such onslaught. A Confederate advance by torchlight at the Battle of Franklin ended in a decisive loss for Cheatham. Worse still was General Stonewall Jackson's scouting expedition in 1863 during the Battle of Chancellorsville to investigate the possibility of launching a night advance. Mistaken for an enemy scout, Jackson was shot and died days later from aggravated pneumonia, a loss that many historians argued doomed Lee's chances at Gettysburg.

The creation of illumination flares and tracer bullets helped to improve the accuracy of night firing during World War I. In so doing, these inventions also helped to negate the one advantage of night combat, its ability to reduce casualties on the attacking side. Perhaps due in part to this, the war saw only limited launching of night raids, and few to no major darkness-aided offensives. An early attempt by the Germans to attack the fortress of Liege at night in August of 1914 was decisively beaten back by the Belgians, while a British night attack at Festubert the next year gained only limited ground at the loss of over sixteen thousand men. These early attempts did much to dissuade both sides from launching massive nocturnal offensives. Instead night raids on trenches and peaceful penetration of outposts became more standard practices, especially among the allies. As late as August of 1918 an Australian attempt to capture Mont Saint-Quentin at night ultimately failed, though a subsequent attack during the day resulted in its fall.

Technological advances during World War II again aided in both the development of increased night actions as well as defenses against it. Radar allowed for the increased bombing at night of precise targets, whereas German zeppelins in World War I could at best bombard large cities and even then without much precision. At the same time night raids undertaken by Allied special forces units led the Germans to employ tripwire flares. Similar equipment helped to cripple an American attempt to cross the Gari River in Italy at the Battle of the Rapido in early 1944.[58]

Night fighting became perfected during the Korean War. Faced with the technological superiority of American and other allied forces, North Korean and Chinese soldiers utilized night marches and nighttime attacks in order to stress and penetrate enemy lines. Supplies were also transported by night to limit the effectiveness of allied air operations. Both sides learned much from these types of operation and when combined with the introduction of night vision scopes led to the standardization of night combat in Vietnam a decade later. Though the majority of these engagements were still small scale, by the time of the Persian Gulf War in 1991 the belligerents would conduct even full-scale battles at night.

One of the more interesting contemporary impacts of the moon upon warfare came on October 5, 1960 when the United States' Ballistic Missile Early Warning System at Thule in Greenland had bounced a signal off of the rising moon, mistaking it for a Soviet nuclear launch.[59] General Laurence Kuter, who was stationed at NORAD in Colorado at the time, quickly identified the error and corrected for it. Even with the advent of modern science and technology, the interference of the heavens remains a factor in modern warfare.

Thanks to concerns about casualties and the availability of technological advances, modern military forces have moved far beyond a fear of battles at night. The knowledge that civilians will also be concentrated in homes at this time rather than out in public places also makes night attacks more effective at both reducing civilian casualties and at identifying enemy forces. Finally, both advanced and primitive forces view nighttime attacks as a combat advantage. Advanced nations see the tactic as allowing them to utilize their technology while more basic nations and rebel groups seek to use it to negate some of the technology of their enemy.

3

RAIN

For after seven more days, I will send rain on the earth
forty days and forty nights; and I will blot out from the
face of the land every living thing that I have made.
—GENESIS 7:4

IT IS PERHAPS TELLING THAT THE great environmental force used by so
many gods to destroy the world, not only for the ancient Hebrews but
many other cultures as well, was rain. Both symbolically and as a force
of destruction, water has the inherent ability to both devastate and
cleanse an area. In terms of warfare, rain produces the two main negative impacts of weather on combat: Hindrance of movement and the
spread of disease. In addition, unlike various rare astronomical phenomena or other forms of location- and climate-restricted weather, rain
is universally present over almost the entire globe. Consequently, rain
has frequently impacted the course of wars throughout human history.

Two of the oldest military-themed epics in world literature, the
Mahabharata and the *Iliad*, both feature rain as components of their
stories. Indra, the Hindu god of rain and war, is featured prominently
in the former tale, in which at one point the hero Drona was told by
Bhishma to "Strong your bow, Brahmana! And what on the bow-
string? The hurricane winds, the snow and the sleet, the shattering

rain, the hot fire—the illusions of war that burn and drown?"[60] Likewise, the *Iliad*, after describing the immense, impenetrable wall built by the Achaeans to guard their ships, alludes to the fact that the wall will ultimately be destroyed by the gods once the war has finished. Each deity will unleash his weapons against the construction with only Zeus having some effect, "while Jove rained the whole time that he might wash it sooner into the sea."[61] Meanwhile four books later, Zeus showered the armies with, "a rain of blood upon the earth in honor of his son whom Patroclus was about to kill on the rich plain of Troy far from his home."[62] Far from simple poetic license, the particular phenomenon that spread so much fear among the combatants may refer to an actual weather event. Fine sand or red algae can be blown up into the lower atmosphere and then combine with rain to produce the phenomenon of "red rain."[63]

The Bible also vividly relates the impact of rain on battle during the judgeship of Deborah. King Jabin of Canaan had oppressed Israel for many years before Deborah and Barak moved to stop him. The battle that followed took place at Mount Tabor in the Jezreel Valley. Although outnumbered by the enemy under Sisera, who was able to muster hundreds of heavy chariots, the Israelites had a far greater ally on their side. The Bible simply records that, "Barak went down Mount Tabor, with ten thousand men following him. At Barak's advance, the Lord routed Sisera and all his chariots and army by the sword, and Sisera got down from his chariot and fled on foot."[64] More information as to how the Israelites were able to overcome such a powerful force comes from both the "Song of Debora" as well as the later historian Flavius Josephus. The former mentions that, "The torrent Kishon swept them away, the onrushing torrent, the torrent Kishon. March on, my soul, with might," while the latter wrote that, "there came down from heaven a great storm, with a vast quantity of rain and hail, and the wind blew the rain in the face of the Canaanites, and so darkened their eyes, that their arrows and slings were of no advantage to them."[65] Flash flooding is known to be an historical occurrence within the Jezreel Valley. A sudden and concentrated rain storm could have certainly created a situation where the heavy chariots of the Canaanites became bogged down or useless in the muddy terrain, thus giving the advantage to the lighter Israeli troops. The same scenario unfolded many years later when a Turkish army, recently defeated by Napoleon and Jean Baptiste Kléber at the Battle of Mount Tabor, saw many of its men killed while retreating, due to flooding in the Wadi Kishon.

The Persian Wars, once again, proved to be as markedly impacted by the element of rain as they had been by heavenly phenomena. The Persian Empire had previously extended its reach into Europe in 512 BC, subjugating the Aegean coast of Thrace. Now, following Greek encouragement of and involvement in the Ionian Revolt, Emperor Darius sent a punitive force to both once again secure the region and to punish Athens and Eretria. As the great armada rounded Mount Athos at the eastern edge of the Chalcidice . . .

> Crossing over from Thasos they travelled near the land as far as Acanthus, and putting out from there they tried to round Athos. But a great and irresistible north wind fell upon them as they sailed past and dealt very roughly with them, driving many of their ships upon Athos. It is said that about three hundred ships were lost, and more than twenty thousand men. Since the coasts of Athos abound in wild beasts, some men were carried off by beasts and so perished; others were dashed against the rocks; those who could not swim perished because of that, and still others by the cold.[66]

A storm in the Aegean accomplished what the Ionians and native Thracians could not, crippling the Persian fleet and forcing Mardonius to eventually withdraw back to Asia. The disaster compelled the emperor to approach the Greek states diplomatically instead, asking for their submission the next year. The refusal of many of the polities to comply forced him to launch a second, larger invasion in 490 BC. Fear of sailing around the northern Aegean led this next expedition's leaders to follow a much more southerly route. The Persian fleet sailed past Rhodes before landing at Samos and Naxos in the calmer waters of the Cyclades. Yet, this more carefully planned invasion was still frustrated in its attempts at the Battle of Marathon. If the earlier attempt had succeeded in its aims, it's likely that the pro-Persian ruler of Athens, the tyrant Hippias, would have offered little resistance and thus markedly changed European history.

Xerxes launched the final Persian attempt to humiliate and subjugate the Greeks in 480 BC. In the late summer of that year, as the Persian army was engaged at Thermopylae, its navy rounded Magnesia as part of an effort to support the land-based force. Herodotus recorded that:

> They spent the night in this way, but at dawn a storm descended upon them out of a clear and windless sky, and the sea began to boil. A strong east wind blew, which the people living in those parts call Hellespontian. Those who felt the wind rising or had proper mooring dragged their ships up on shore ahead of the storm and so survived with their ships. The wind did, however, carry those ships caught out in the open sea against the rocks called the Ovens at Pelion or onto the beach. Some ships were wrecked on the Sepian headland, others were cast ashore at the city of Meliboea or at Casthanaea. The storm was indeed unbearable . . . They say that at the very least no fewer than four hundred ships were destroyed in this labor, along with innumerable men and abundant wealth.[67]

The three-day storm devastated the Persian navy, yet its immense size enabled it to continue its course down the coast of Euboea. During the ensuing three-day Battle of Artemisium, the Persian fleet was again struck by a storm.

> To those who were appointed to sail round Euboea, however, that same night was still more cruel since it caught them on the open sea.

Their end was a terrible one, for when the storm and the rain came
on them in their course off the Hollows of Euboea, they were driven
by the wind in an unknown direction and were driven onto the rocks.
All this was done by the god so that the Persian power might be more
equally matched with the Greek, and not much greater than it.[68]

Though in the end the Greeks were unable to stop the Persian army
at Thermopylae or its navy at Artemisium, both served to delay and
degrade the enemy invasion force. The storms at Magnesia and Artemisium especially served to drastically reduce the overall size of Xerxes's fleet to the point that the Greeks were able to defeat it at Salamis
shortly afterward. Fear of additional weather-related disasters also
helped to convince the emperor to withdraw the rest of his fleet back
to Asia Minor.

The decades-long stalemate of the Peloponnesian War owed many
of its turning points to the interactions of weather and warfare. As
many of these engagements principally concerned the open sea, wind
and rain proved to be some of the most formidable challenges faced
by the Athenians and Spartans. The war is generally considered to
have started with a Theban attempt to extend its influence over Plataea. Utilizing a storm and a moonless night, a small force of Thebans
managed to infiltrate the city, demanding it immediately ally with
their government. Unfortunately, the small size of the invasion force
meant that the local Plataean population was soon able to overcome
the soldiers and retake their own city. The very storm that the Thebans
utilized to enter the town also served to hasten their demise as the
flooded river Asopos kept reinforcements from reaching the besieged
Thebans. The Plataeans used a similar tactic to attempt a breakout
from their besieged town in 427 BC. Following an elaborate yearlong
siege of their city by Sparta, several hundred soldiers decided to conduct an audacious sortie in order to escape to Athens. They chose the
night of a particularly heavy storm to carry out their operation, with
even Thucydides recognizing that, "it was mainly the violence of the

storm that enabled them to affect their escape at all."[69] Gaius Carrinas undertook a similar operation almost four centuries later in 82 BC, when he found himself besieged after being defeated by Pompey and Marcus Crassus near Spoletium. Utilizing a tremendous rainstorm one night, Carrinas was able to safely evacuate his men.[70] A generation before, the onset of a violent rainstorm saved a Roman army under Gnaeus Carbo from utter annihilation after a devastating defeat by the Cimbri at the Battle of Noreia. The well-timed storm and a subsequent strategic mistake by the Germans in marching toward Gaul rather than into the Italian peninsula, helped to save the city of Rome from conquest.

Likewise, in the year 173 AD, the Quadi hemmed in a Roman army while fighting in Germany. Only the "Miracle of the Rain" is alleged to have saved both the army and Emperor Marcus Aurelius. The Roman historian Cassius Dio described the event:

> For when the Romans were in peril in the course of the battle, the divine power saved them in a most unexpected manner. The Quadi had surrounded them at a spot favorable for their purpose and the Romans were fighting valiantly with their shields locked together; then the barbarians ceased fighting, expecting to capture them easily as the result of the heat and their thirst. So they posted guards all about and hemmed them in to prevent their getting water anywhere; for the barbarians were far superior in numbers. The Romans, accordingly, were in a terrible plight from fatigue, wounds, the heat of the sun, and thirst, and so could neither fight nor retreat, but were standing and the line and at their several posts, scorched by the heat, when suddenly many clouds gathered and a mighty rain, not without divine interposition, burst upon them. Indeed, there is a story to the effect that Arnuphis, an Egyptian magician, who was a companion of Marcus, had invoked by means of enchantments various deities and in particular Mercury, the god of the air, and by this means attracted the rain.[71]

A latter commentator on Dio agreed with the order of historical events but credited the intercession to the Christian God.

> When Marcus found himself at a loss what to do in the circumstances and feared for his whole army, the prefect approached him and told him that those who are called Christians can accomplish anything whatever by their prayers and that in the army there chanced to be a whole division of this sect. Marcus on hearing this appealed to them to pray to their God; and when they had prayed, their God immediately gave ear and smote the enemy with a thunderbolt and comforted the Romans with a shower of rain. Marcus was greatly astonished at this and not only honoured the Christians by an official decree but also named the legion the "thundering" Legion.[72]

Various naval assaults were also impacted by the unpredictable storms that would periodically emerge in the Aegean Sea. The Athenian general Phormio won great victories at Rhium and Naupactus in 429 BC with his tactical innovation and personal daring as the promised Athenian reinforcements had been delayed at Crete due to a storm. Around the same time, a powerful thunderstorm likewise frustrated a Spartan attempt to send an expedition to Lesbos. One such rainstorm, in fact, helped to produce one of the most crushing Spartan defeats of the entire conflict. Eschewing Pericles's Fabian strategy of wearing down the strength and position of the Peloponnesians, the Athenians dispatched a fleet in 425 BC to begin harassing enemy interests on the Adriatic coast of Greece. Demosthenes, an officer in the fleet, favored fortifying a permanent position in the region, but was overruled by the expedition's leaders. A chance storm forced the ships to seek refuge at Pylos and the Athenians began to fortify their position out of both boredom and fear of attack. When the Spartans heard of the landing they sent a larger fleet with hundreds of soldiers to expel Demosthenes. The ensuing battle not only witnessed the destruction of much of the Spartan navy but the surrounding and isolation of 120 Spartiates, the elite of Spartan society, on the island of Sphacteria. Demosthenes's storm off of Pylos completely altered the path of the war, leading to Athenian dominance for years and forcing Sparta to agree to the Peace of Nicias by 421 BC.

Spartan strategy for victory in the Peloponnesian War eventually hinged upon control of the Bosporus in order to cut off Athens's grain supply from the Black Sea region. The area had long been a focal point for Greek expansion, itself often interconnecting with weather. According to ancient Greek mythology, King Cyzicus once welcomed Jason and the Argonauts in the region as they sailed for Colchis. Tragically their subsequent departure was marred by a massive rainstorm and thick fog which drove the heroes' ship back toward Cyzicus and resulted in an unintentional battle during which the king was killed. Hundreds of years later, in 410 BC, the Spartans managed to seize the town of Cyzicus and began the process of restricting Athenian access to the Black Sea. In response, Alcibiades sailed with eighty-six triremes toward the Hellespont in an attempt to surprise and defeat the enemy. Under cover of a sudden storm, the Athenian general was able to approach the anchored Spartan contingent and draw them out into battle. At this point additional Athenian units appeared on the enemy's flanks and produced a stunning victory for Alcibiades. Athenian control of the region was secured for another four years and seemed to presage an end to the conflict.

Despite renewed Spartan efforts in Asia Minor, the Athenians were able to maintain dominance for a number of years. Even after Conon's fleet was trapped at Mytilene, a hastily constructed relief force was able to crush the Spartan navy at Arginusae. Yet, the victory was tempered by what occurred afterward. The onset of a storm, when combined with the fact that Conon's ships were still under threat at Mytilene, led the Athenian commanders to disregard the rescue of their fellow citizens from the twenty-five wrecked triremes. Upon their return to Athens, the fury of the populace resulted in the execution of six out of the eight generals. Though a great victory had been secured, the subsequent storm decimated the ranks of Athenian leadership, hastening its defeat at Aegospotami, and its loss of the war shortly afterward.

Rain and wetness have always had a debilitating effect on metal tools and weapons, though this often is a long-term impact. Yet more delicate materials, such as rope and wood, can be harmed almost immediately. Such was the case at the Battle of Teutoburg Forest, where torrential rain and incessant fog wreaked havoc on the equipment of the besieged Romans. As discussed in the previous chapter, the Romans had established a fortified camp during the night following the initial attack by the German tribes. Night rains rendered the defenders' bows useless in their subsequent breakout attempt. Worse yet, the soldiers' shields, composed of glued wood wrapped in cloth or leather, became waterlogged and unmanageable, leaving the Romans vulnerable to the missiles and weapons of the enemy. German weather allied with German warriors to defeat the invading army and permanently secure the independence of the region.

A similar fate befell Oda Nobunaga in 1573 as he attempted to take Nagashima for the second time. Though he carefully maneuvered his gunners toward the fortress, a sudden heavy downpour soaked the gunpowder and matches of his men, rendering almost all of his matchlock guns useless. A quick counterattack by the Ikkō-ikki scattered his men and almost cost him his life as well. Around the same time in late 1524, a French army under King Francis I attempted to assault the strategic city of Pavia during its invasion of Italy. Unfortunately, the onset of rainy weather ruined gunpowder supplies, hampered movement, spread misery and disease, and prevented the successful taking of the city. Instead, the French monarch was forced to settle down to a siege of the town. As the months dragged on Spanish reinforcement arrived and on February 24, 1525, Charles de Lannoy launched a surprise attack on the French position. Not only was the enemy army massacred, but Francis I himself was captured. Rainy weather ended a century of French hopes in the peninsula and cemented Habsburg dominance over central Europe.

Besides simply weapons, heavy rain could also foul terrain, alter the best-laid plans, and increase the difficulty of combat. In the case of the Roman city of Aurelianum (Orleans), it even saved the lives of the population. Attila the Hun drove into Gaul in AD 451, burning and pillaging all in his path. His army quickly overran and occupied the region from the Rhine to the Seine, and by the end of May he had reached the important city of Aurelianum on the Loire River. Though promised entrance to the city by the local ruler, Attila instead found the gates barred and its inhabitants prepared for siege. Days of heavy rain dragged the siege on much longer than the Huns could afford to waste, and by the time the walls were finally breached on June 14, reports of an approaching German-Roman army led Attila to abandon his attack and quickly move eastward to the Catalaunian Plains. Not only was the city of Orleans saved from massacre, but the subsequent battle saw the defeat of Attila and the salvation of Rome.

At the start of the first century AD, Wang Mang ruled China and what was seen as the illegitimate Xin Dynasty. Numerous agrarian, religious, and political rebellions erupted to overthrow the monarch. In keeping with the Chinese political philosophy of the Mandate of Heaven, especially as formulated by Dong Zhongshu, any disturbances in nature could be viewed as evidence of heaven's displeasure with the ruler. This worldview would pay particular dividends for the Lulin rebels following their confrontation with imperial soldiers at the Battle of Kunyang in AD 23. After battling the Xin for six years, forces loyal to the former Han Dynasty were surrounded and besieged in the city of Kunyang. While the arrival of reinforcements and a breakout attempt managed to defeat a portion of the Xin army, a sudden flash flood caused by torrential rains devastated the imperial camp and killed thousands of fleeing soldiers. News of the disaster prompted further uprisings across China and led to the death of Wang Mang and the restoration of the Han.

In portions of the globe that experienced rainy seasons, warfare, much like farming, became scheduled around these predictable deluges. Failure to understand and appreciate this rhythm of nature could result in disaster. Such was the case in the last few years of the sixth century during the Sui Dynasty's invasion of Korea. The three-hundred-thousand-man Chinese army marched into Manchuria in August and was almost immediately confronted by the annual torrential rains that affected the region. Mired in mud, with supplies becoming ruined, and disease breaking out among the soldiers, the vast majority of the invasion force became casualties. The storms likewise served to wreck most of the accompanying navy under Zhou Luohou, leading to its subsequent defeat at the Battle of the Bohai Sea. The massive failure of the expedition overall, with its tremendous costs in both treasure and manpower, became one of the prime reasons for the downfall of the entire Sui Dynasty only a few years later.

Indochina had its military history affected by rainy seasons perhaps more than any other area on the planet. The various Burmese-Siamese Wars of the sixteenth to nineteenth centuries were frequently interrupted due to seasonal flooding, especially around the region of the capital city of Ayutthaya. Even Europeans fighting in the region were powerless to confront the yearly rains, as Englishman James McCarthy discovered in the latter half of the nineteenth century during the Haw Wars. The rainy season brought malaria, a foe that was more feared by the English than the weapons of the Haw Chinese.

Henry Stafford, Second Duke of Buckingham, experienced one of the defining characteristics of rain—its effect on movement—seeing his carefully planned rebellion derailed due to an unexpected storm and subsequent flooding. Rising up against King Richard III in 1483, Buckingham was to cross the River Severn and march on London as Henry Tudor landed in the east with soldiers from Brittany. Despite careful planning and the support of both Welsh and English lords, a series of storms struck the area in October, effectively defeating the rebellion for Richard III. Buckingham's river crossing could not be carried out due to the flooding of both the Severn and the surrounding region, allowing the King to move his forces west and contain the uprising. At the same time, storms drove Henry Tudor's invasion force back to France, ruining any chance of Buckingham receiving reinforcements. Though the rebellion was ultimately a failure, its very existence helped to inspire further uprisings against Richard, which would soon lead to his overthrow and death only two years later.

Four hundred years later wet and rainy conditions in the west of England also helped to delay and demoralize the rebellion of the Duke of Monmouth. After landing in southwestern England in June of 1685, Monmouth was able to rapidly take Taunton where he conducted a coronation. However, as he moved against Bristol, worsening weather and severe rain slowed down his disorganized army. Eventually he was forced to abandon the siege and take shelter from the drenching storm. It was at this point that Royalist troops arrived and drove Monmouth away from the city. A litany of minor skirmishes combined with harsh weather to break the discipline of Monmouth's hastily assembled army. Cornered at the Battle of Sedgemoor, his army was unable to hold back the onslaught of the Earl of Eversham. As summarized years later, "Their numbers had now been thinned by desertions; they had suffered by the weather; their money was nearly spent, and they paid for nothing, but lived at free quarter upon the inhabitants."[73]

Movement became an even trickier proposition with the advent of heavy cavalry forces, full metal armor, and bulky artillery. Prior to the era of modern road construction, European forces especially were at the mercy of weather, muddy fields, and thousand-year-old Roman roads. In 1415, King Henry V of England invaded France in an effort to restart the stalled Hundred Years' War. Though outnumbered and outclassed by the heavy cavalry of the French army at the Battle of Agincourt, the English monarch expected to utilize the layout of the battlefield as well as his longbowmen to even the odds. What was perhaps unplanned for by Henry however, was the two-week-long series of rainstorms that turned most of freshly ploughed northeastern France into a mire of mud. The dismounted French knights found their movement slowed to a crawl, giving greater time for the English archers to devastate their ranks. As a monk at St. Denis reported several years later, the knights were "marching through the middle of the mud where they sank up to their knees. So they were already overcome with fatigue even before they advanced against the enemy."[74] Thousands of the best knights in France were killed, either succumbing to flights of arrows or drowning in the foot-deep mud.

Exactly eighty years later a similar situation confronted the French, this time in the Italian peninsula. After a lightning campaign southward from France to Naples in 1485, Charles VIII was compelled to return home to Paris after the formation of the Holy League by various Italian states to oppose him. Fearing being cut off, Charles left a small garrison in Naples and slowly retraced his steps back toward the Alps. By early July he had reached the town of Fornovo on the Taro river when he encountered the main League army under Marquis Francesco II Gonzago of Mantua. Not wanting to engage the Italian troops on their chosen ground and fearing the large number of heavy cavalry on the opposite side, Charles VIII astutely crossed the Taro. A series of heavy rains were beginning to swell the stream and soon created a formidable barrier between the two armies. The French movement disrupted Gonzago's plans, and forced him to bring his horse across the river and up its slippery slopes to assault the French lines. Though Charles lost almost all of his treasure in a Venetian raid on his baggage train, he was able to hold the field and continue his withdrawal to France. The rain-swollen river had saved the monarch's army from almost certain destruction.

A similar fate befell the Mongol invasion of Hungary in 1241 as well as an Ottoman army under Sultan Suleiman I as it besieged Vienna in 1529. In the case of the Turks, they had begun moving through the Balkans in late spring, encountering the full brunt of the rains that swept the region at that time of year. Not only did rain-augmented disease begin to decimate his ranks, but the Turkish supply camels became casualties to the weather and road conditions as well. With increasingly impassable roads and fields, Suleiman was eventually forced to abandon his heavy artillery also, dooming the attack from the start. The actual attack began in September and continued on into October. The arrival of more wet weather led the Sultan to attempt one final assault, which ultimately failed. Niklas I, Graf zu Salm's Imperial army, though outnumbered by perhaps ten to one, was enabled by the wet weather to establish the high tide of Ottoman power in Europe. In 1709 a similar bout of wet weather rendered the artillery of Charles XII of Sweden largely ineffective before the pivotal Battle of Poltava, ending that nation's century-long rise to global prominence and shifting power in eastern Europe toward Russia instead.

An army that could successfully adjust to difficult weather conditions often proved to be victorious in combat. Such was the case of the Spanish army at the Siege of Baza in 1489. Ferdinand and Isabella had launched the final war to reconquer the Iberian Peninsula in 1487 by invading Granada. After winning the majority of the kingdom, the Spanish army set down to besiege the fortress of Baza. Though formidable in its own right, the Muslim defenders of the castle were also counting on the arrival of the autumn rains to devastate the camps of the besieging Castilian army. As retold by Washington Irving, "Mohammed Ibn Hassan . . . endeavored to rally the spirits of the prince. 'The rainy season is at hand . . . the floods will soon pour down from the mountains; the rivers will overflow their banks and inundate the valleys . . . a single wintry storm from our mountains would wash away his canvas city."[75] Rather than be driven off by the rains of the region, the Spanish began to rebuild their temporary siege camp into a permanent city of wood, stone, and terracotta. The determination of the besiegers paid off as the prince of Baza, Cid Hiaya, soon after accepted an offer of surrender. A commitment to take the city regardless of the costs, and knowledge of local weather conditions, had enabled victory for the Spanish as much as by the power of their arms. Rodrigo Ponce de León's seizure of Alhama in 1481 and the Moorish conquest of Zahara the same year, both in heavy rainstorms, further show that armies familiar with the weather of a region are little affected by it.

Ironically, Ferdinand and Isabella would not have sat on the throne together, nor would Spain have united in the manner that it did, had it not been for a massive rainstorm in 1476. The War of Castilian Succession which raged from 1475 to 1479 pitted Isabella, the half sister of the previous monarch, against Joanna, his alleged illegitimate daughter. The deciding point of the conflict was the Battle of Toro, which took place in March of 1476. Afonso V of Portugal marched his army to besiege Ferdinand of Aragon in the important city of Zamora in February of that year. Yet days of heavy rain and cold weather so demoralized his army and made preparations so difficult, that Afonso gave up the siege and withdrew back to Portugal. One chronicler recorded that the men, "suffered much rain, cold and snow from which they suffered so much loss."[76] Ferdinand seized upon the opportunity and followed the enemy, engaging Afonso at Toro. Thought the subsequent battle was largely inconclusive, Afonso followed it up by completely withdrawing from Spain while numerous supporters of Joanna now began to back Isabella. The War of Castilian Succession would drag on for several more years, yet Toro would mark the last chance for a Portuguese conquest of part of Spain.

A century later around the other side of the globe a Japanese army likewise made good use of a rainstorm to defeat an enemy. Imagawa Yoshimoto was marching a large army against Kyoto in 1560, passing first through Owari Province. Oda Nobunaga had only just recently unified that territory and resolved to stop Imagawa if possible. Outnumbered by ten to one, Oda decided to launch a surprise attack on the enemy camp, catching them unexpected. As he proceeded to move his three thousand men through the forest to the north of the camp, a tremendous thunderstorm suddenly broke out. Imagawa's men huddled together to avoid the rain as best they could. Suddenly, as the storm cleared, Oda's army rushed into the camp and slaughtered most of the enemy army, including Imagawa himself. Oda Nobunaga emerged from the battle, thanks to a timely storm, as one of the leading warlords of Japan. Yet, fortune and weather are fickle, and as described above, a subsequent assault by Oda in 1573 against Nagashima fortress failed when a rainstorm soaked the guns and powder of his men.

The French under Marshal Soult repeated Oda's tactic in 1809 during their retreat from Portugal. Finding themselves harassed by English cavalry to their rear and blocked by the partially dismantled Ponte Nova in front of them, Soult sent Major Dulong with a handful of men across the bare beams of the bridge. "The rain fell heavily . . . the torrents descending from the mountains, and the Cavado itself made such a noise, that the march of the French was not heard."[77] Thanks to the cover of the rain, the daring Dulong was able to cross the bridge, kill the sentries on the other side, and exfiltrate Soult's entire force.

The Siege of Namur in 1692 took place from May 25 to June 30, 1692, and saw both sides heavily impacted by a series of massive rainstorms. The French experienced great difficulties in moving supplies to and from the siege, especially their heavier guns and ammunition. Disease and depravation struck both camps as supplies became waterlogged and fodder nonexistent. The worst result of the flooding and muddy terrain though was its effect on an English relief army under William III of England. Marching toward Namur, the English force became blocked by the flooding Mehaigne River and proved unable to support the trapped Spanish soldiers. By the end of June, Louis XIV had taken the fortress of Namur and secured a major victory in the Nine Years' War.

The turning point of the American Revolution is usually considered to have come at the Battle of Saratoga in the fall of 1777. Following the loss of New York and New Jersey, there was mounting pressure on the Americans to achieve a decisive victory. This was especially needed if there was to be any hope of securing an alliance with France or any one of the other great European powers. The British campaign in New York had aimed, through a three-pronged invasion, to capture Albany and thus divide New England from the rest of the colonies. Though Barry St. Ledger's advance down the Mohawk had faltered and William Howe had decided to not march up the Hudson, preferring instead to take

Philadelphia, John Burgoyne still moved with determination down the Hudson from Canada. A series of battles with American forces under the command of Horatio Gates and Benedict Arnold eventual killed or wounded 1,100 men out of the 7,200-man British-German force, yet the real victory was to come several days later. Following his defeat on October 7, 1777, Burgoyne wisely ordered a withdrawal north toward the safety of Fort Ticonderoga. Unfortunately, heavy rains made the roads and region into fields of mud, slowing his movement to a crawl. In fact, over the course of the next two days Burgoyne was only able to cover nine miles, reaching the village of Saratoga. Once the American units had caught up to the English they successfully surrounded his army, eventually compelling Burgoyne to surrender his entire force by October 15. The rains of upstate New York had served as an auxiliary arm of the American rebellion, helping to secure a French alliance shortly afterward. Yet they were not always so favorable to the Patriot cause, as terrible rainstorms left over from the Independence Hurricane of 1775 delayed the American assault on Fort St. Jean, dooming the campaign against Quebec.

Rain also aided in helping to spread contagion, inducing privation among soldiers in the field as occurred at numerous sieges during the Dutch Revolt. During the American Revolution, General Cornwallis was particularly hard-hit by this during his campaign in the Southern colonies. Close to two-thirds of his men would eventually succumb to illnesses such as dysentery, yellow fever, and malaria, most made prevalent by the heat and rains of the region.[78] Washington himself blamed the wet weather on Long Island for the weakening of his army shortly before his loss to the British in August of 1776. "The weather of late has been extremely wet . . . which has occasioned much sickness, and the men to be almost broke down."[79] In a similar fashion, the Duke of Brunswick's retreat after the disastrous Battle of Valmy in 1792 saw his soldiers beset by dysentery following the onset of the autumnal rains. Likewise, the British army was devastated by malarial fever in the Netherlands while campaigning there in 1809 due to similar conditions.

Perhaps the most famous example occurred at the start of Napoleon's invasion of Russia, when upon crossing the Niemen River his troops were inundated by a series of rain storms and westerly winds. These undoubtedly helped to create the conditions that began the emergence of contagion among his men, the ultimate conqueror of his army.

In fact, weather proved to be one of the few enemies that Napoleon Bonaparte could not defeat. During his campaign in northern Italy in 1796, the young general found himself confronted by an entrenched Austrian foe at Mantua and two approaching relief armies. In an effort to defeat one of the latter forces, Napoleon led an assault on the Austrian position at Caldiero. As his men advanced a tremendous rainstorm poured down that not only hampered their movement but also fouled their gunpowder and muskets. In addition, as the fields quickly turned to mud the French cannons were unable to be moved forward and utilized against the entrenched Austrian positions. By the end of the day Napoleon was forced to withdraw; a rare defeat for the great leader caused more by weather than by the generalship of the Austrians. A decade later, a French assault on the town of Tarifa in 1812 was frustrated due to a similar rainstorm. The outnumbered British and Spanish defenders were able to hold out and Victor and Soult soon after gave up their siege of nearby Cadiz. Nor was snow the only elemental enemy that Napoleon had to deal with during his invasion of Russia. Following his retreat from Moscow and subsequent German campaign that would end at Leipzig, Napoleon saw one of his armies defeated at Katzbach more by rain than by battle. The French commander himself, Marshal MacDonald, wrote that due to the rain, "the state of affairs was so disheartening that I ordered a retreat."[80] Nor was rain simply a hindrance to movement or promoter of disease. In September of 1813 a force of two thousand Turkish soldiers camped near the Danube at Vidin drowned when the rain-swollen river suddenly overwhelmed their encampment. Lord Byron himself, fighting close by in Greece in 1824, came down with a fever after traveling and fighting in the rain of the region. Already suffering from malaria, he died just over a week later.

Many writers and historians have even posited that were it not for rain, Napoleon would not have lost at Waterloo in 1815.[81] On the night of June 17, a torrential rainstorm struck the area of Belgium, turning the field at Waterloo into a quagmire. Napoleon had spent many years utilizing his artillery to its fullest advantage in order to defeat his enemy. Yet, to accomplish that this time, he was forced to wait for hours while the ground slowly dried out, otherwise his heavy artillery would have become unmovable over the muddy fields. This delay until nearly noon meant that the battle was still raging as the Prussian army arrived at 4:30 PM to deliver the final blow to the French. Rain had once again halted the ambitions of the French emperor.

Rain impacted one of the most infamous slave revolts in American history as well. Gabriel, a literate and skilled slave in Virginia, organized a large slave revolt in 1800 allegedly with backing from various religious and Jeffersonian groups. All that prevented a potential slaughter, or forced emancipation in the state was a torrential rainstorm that delayed Gabriel's planned uprising. Local planters were able to discover the plot and Gabriel himself was eventually turned over and executed. What followed was a significant hardening of views toward slaves and a limiting of freedoms for both slaves and freedmen.

The American Civil War experienced a number of rain-related battles and marches that, with the number of men involved, presaged similar events in Europe in 1914. Restrictions on movement remained one of the key impacts of rain as tens of thousands of men and camp followers attempted to trek across the muddy fields and rural roads of the South. Perhaps the most disastrous was the doomed Mud March of January 1863. Following his devastating attempt to push Lee from Fredericksburg in December of 1862, Gen. Ambrose Burnside moved to launch a new offensive in January of the next year. Unbeknownst to the Union commander, just as his men were preparing to break camp and march toward the river a massive nor'easter was bearing down on the coast of Virginia. Torrents of rain fell from January 20–22, leaving the Union army stuck in a sea of mud. Col. Regis de Trobriand wrote later that:

> The rain lasted thirty hours without cessation. To understand the effect, one must have lived in Virginia through a winter. The roads are nothing but dirt roads. The mud is not simply on the surface, but penetrates the ground to a great depth. It appears as though the water, after passing through a first bed of clay, soaked into some kind of earth without any consistency. As soon as the hardened crust on the surface is softened, everything is buried in a sticky paste mixed with liquid mud, in which, with my own eyes, I have seen teams of mules buried.[82]

Unable to continue, Burnside turned his army around and struggled to return to camp. The entire operation proved to be a disaster and a thoroughly disgusted Lincoln went on to fire the general two days later. Burnside's predecessor, George McClellan, had used rainy weather as an excuse to cover his own lack of progress during the Peninsula Campaign a year before. Lincoln had seen through his ruse and eventually replaced him with Burnside.

The first major Union victory of the war and the fate of Kentucky were also secured through the presence of rain. Despite initial attempts by the border state to remain neutral, first Confederate and then Union forces soon violated its territory in September of 1861. Southern troops in the state under the command of Albert Sidney Johnston were in the process of repositioning and strengthening their lines when a Union army under George H. Thomas marched against them. General Felix Kirck Zollicoffer, who was in command of the extreme right wing of Johnston's army, had mistakenly camped for the winter with his back to the Cumberland River. The newly appointed Crittenden and General Johnston saw the danger that could develop should the Union drive south and trap Zollicoffer against the river. Though the Tennessean balked at the subsequent order to march his troops west toward

Crittenden at Mill Springs south of the Cumberland, his greater problem was a lack of boats to ferry his men across the melting snow and rain-swollen river. While heavy rains also delayed the Union advance toward the river, it was to be the weapons of both sides that helped to decide the victor. The ensuing Battle of Mill Springs, fought on January 19, 1862, saw frequent downpours and waterlogged fields. The antiquated flintlocks of many of the Southern soldiers proved either unreliable or useless due to the weather.[83] Thomas's forces were able to repel a rebel assault and eventually push the Southerners south off of the field. Zollicoffer himself, wearing a conspicuous white raincoat, was shot and killed by a Northern soldier. Poor strategy and rainy weather helped to cost the South the state of Kentucky and began the slow Union drive down the Mississippi River.

The Confederates were not immune to the rainy and muddy conditions of their home territory though. Lee's withdrawal from Gettysburg threatened to be more disastrous than the battle itself as recent rains had swollen the Potomac and left the normally fordable river a barrier to his army's retreat. The Confederates were forced to dig in, throwing up temporary fortifications in an effort to prevent a massacre should the Union soldiers attack them with the river to their backs. In the end, Meade's reluctance to fight, torrential rains and muddy conditions that delayed the Union army, and sheer providence allowed Lee's men to survive. Meade finally announced the commencement of an attack on July 14, but unbeknownst to him the Potomac had receded enough to allow the Southerners to make it across the night before. A perennially frustrated Lincoln would soon effectively replace Meade in command by moving Grant to Virginia. The Confederates had, at least in part, shown interest in Gettysburg due to its shoe factory. While this was certainly not their primary motivation, the scarcity of adequate footwear for Southern troops was often a reality. In fact, a year later at the Battle of New Market in May of 1864, a Confederate attack across a rain-soaked, muddy field caused hundreds of men to lose their boots in what became known as the "Field of Lost Shoes."

Though rain had almost cost Lee his army after Gettysburg, it had previously helped him to secure what has been termed his most per-fect victory a few months before. As the Southern commander moved north as part of his unfolding campaign to march into Pennsylvania, his army collided with that of Hooker at the Battle of Chancellors-ville. On May 2, 1863, General Jackson led his men on a wide flanking maneuver around the right of the Northern army. The heavy rains of a few days prior had wet the roads and ground enough so that practi-cally no dust was thrown up by his men as they marched. Though he himself would be shot later that night during a reconnaissance, Jack-son's rain-aided maneuver helped to defeat the Union and set the stage for the Gettysburg Campaign that was to follow.

Rain and muddy conditions could on occasion prove to be fatal as well. At the height of the Battle of Chantilly in September of 1862, an engagement already made quite difficult by a soaking thunderstorm, the legendary Union commander Philip Kearny rode into the Confed-erate lines by accident and was shot and killed. The loss of both him and General Stevens as well as the inability of the Union soldiers to pierce the rebel lines due to their many soaked and useless guns, led to a continued withdrawal by Northern forces back toward Washington.

Necessity eventually drove the Union armies to adapt to the often rain-soaked trails and dirt roads that characterized Southern transpor-tation. In sharp contrast to McClellan's feigned impotence before the muddy ground of Virginia, Gen. William Tecumseh Sherman proved quite adept at pushing through Georgia and South Carolina regardless of local conditions. Despite heavy flooding between Columbia and Charleston, his men constructed corduroy road with sand-covered logs to help complete his March to the Sea that caused so much devastation to the Confederacy.

Rain and wet conditions continued to affect combat during the second half of the nineteenth century, most notably at Sadowa in 1866. A war correspondent with the *London Times* described the heavy rain which blanketed the region the night before the battle, venturing to guess that the Prussians would most likely attack that morning as, "they knew their needle-guns would be less injured than the Austrian muzzle-loaders."[84] The reporter went on to comment on the advantage that the former would have due to the fact that during the storm, "nearly all the Austrian army was lying out in the fields, while many of their own men were sheltered in villages." Sure enough, the Prussians were able to score a decisive victory over the Austrians that set in motion the rise of the German Empire.

Likewise, as European and American armies began to travel overseas they were once again thrust into waging war in unfamiliar climates where heavy rains were often associated with tropical diseases. The British blamed just such a connection for their failure in the Second Ashanti War in 1863. In response General Garnet Wolseley planned a lighting campaign to both commence and end before the rainy season for the Third Ashanti War in 1874. To help achieve his goal of reducing the enemy capital in the shortest time possible, Wolseley employed local labor to construct roads and bridges to move his army effectively once it arrived. Thanks to these efforts the expeditionary force began marching on January 1, 1874 and was able to defeat the main Ashanti army, raze its capital, and re-embark on transports for England by March 4. The heaviest rain of the region and its associated diseases were avoided and two decades of relative peace descended on the Gold Coast. Interestingly, the adoption of European weapons by the Ashanti proved to be a weakness in this war as the rains that began to strike in January fouled their flintlock muskets, while the more modern British rifles were unaffected.[85]

The Zulu War tested the ability of the Victorian British army to operate in rainy and flooded conditions. The disaster at Isandlwana in January of 1879 was set in motion, in part, by the flooded conditions confronting Lord Chelmsford's army maneuvers. The movement of the British army was slowed and its original deployment into five columns was reduced by necessity to only three. Swollen rivers also delayed Tucker's relief column in March, which resulted in the ambush of David Moriarty's men at Intombe. Moreover, rainy weather also hampered communications, most notably the heliographs used by the British to transmit signals and information.[86] Finally, the English horses that were shipped to the country also began to suffer from the weather and the associated lack of grazing.[87]

Yet Chelmsford quickly learned from his mistakes, and when he launched a relief column toward Eshowe in April he adjusted his tactics due to both the presence of the Zulu as well as flooded rivers. Laagering his men at every stop, he was able to avoid ambushes and counter the numerical superiority of the Zulu. When the British relief column was finally attacked at Gingindlovu, Chelmsford's tactics combined with the muddy ground to produce a disaster for the African army.

Additional episodes of warfare impacted by rain and flooding include the Boer War at the turn of the century and the Russo-Japanese War in 1904. Yet these were minor incidents compared to the possibilities offered by the trench warfare of Western Europe during World War I. The millions of men who had dug themselves into six-foot-deep dirt trenches quickly realized that rain could be a far more destructive opponent than bullets. The persistent wet and cold conditions that the feet of soldiers were subjected to led to numerous cases of trench foot, many of which led to amputation or even death. The British alone reported twenty thousand cases over the winter of 1914 and 1915. With wetter-than-normal conditions in Western Europe at that time, the stage was set for potential disaster.[88]

In keeping with the example of Sherman half a century prior, armies in the Great War were quick to adapt to changing weather conditions. Duckboards were soon being installed in all trenches to keep the soldiers away from the filth and rain that populated the bottom of their defensive works. British and French soldiers were being issued numerous pairs of socks by late 1915 and were under orders to change them frequently and rub their feet down with either powder or whale oil to prevent trench foot and other moisture-caused conditions.

The rains that fell in eastern France during the year 1916 proved to be one of unsung heroes of the Battle of Verdun. From the initial launch of Operation Judgement to the ultimate failure of the siege by December, German efforts were continuously hampered by rain and flooding. Quite inauspiciously, the opening of the campaign had to be delayed by nine days due to wet conditions on the field. The rain that helped to prevent the Germans from taking Verdun also helped to produce an equally terrible catastrophe for the nation. An abundance of rainfall in the fall effectively ruined the potato and grain crop in Germany, leading to starvation, disease, and a period that became known as the Turnip Winter as civilians were reduced to sparse amounts of food. B. Liddell Hart would later argue that the blockade of the German coast was the primary reason for its defeat in the war, if this is true then it was certainly aided by the rainy autumn of 1916.[89]

Since World War I saw little movement on the battlefield, rains did not often impact larger strategy. This changed though in World War II when the return to large-area campaigns necessitated a proper understanding of weather. Hitler's invasion of the Soviet Union was delayed by five weeks due to the demands of his campaigns elsewhere as well as flooding conditions in the Balkans due to heavy rains. When the attack finally began in late June of 1941, the late summer rainstorms of Belarus periodically slowed the advance. The wet autumns of western Russia further complicated operations, turning the trails and fields before Moscow into mud and slowing the Germans to a crawl. By the time winter set in, Hitler's forces were far from their objectives and exposed. Yet, rain was not always on the side of the Allies, as General Patton and his men had to contend with seven inches of precipitation while fighting to take the city of Metz in late 1944. The American commander's Christmas message reflected the age-old beseeching of divine intervention in order to seek better weather. "Almighty and most merciful Father, we humbly beseech Thee, of Thy great goodness, to restrain these immoderate rains with which we have to contend. Grant us fair weather for battle."

The seasonal weather patterns of Asia again proved to present a strategic consideration during the wars of the late nineteenth and twentieth centuries, especially to outside aggressors. During the Japanese invasion of Korea in 1894, a defeated Chinese army under General Ye Zhichao was able to avoid surrender at Pyongyang by utilizing a rainstorm to cover its retreat back over the Yalu River. During the Korean War, the North launched its initial offensive at the start of the monsoon season, no doubt in a bid to reduce enemy air operations and to hamper the South's ability to withdraw its men as fields quickly became quagmires. As the conflict reduced itself to the trench warfare reminiscent of World War I, the monsoon rains brought on disease, depression, and death.

The situation worsened during the French and American campaigns in Vietnam a decade later. A warmer climate and more active monsoon season exaggerated the challenges that had been faced in Korea in the 1950s. French efforts at Dien Bien Phu were severely hampered by the onset of the monsoonal rains, which not only flooded the defensive works but reduced air support as well. As the French had first explored the region during the dry season, they underestimated the impact that the rains would have on their operation. With a heavy reliance on both airpower and air mobility, the American army also found themselves confronted by the environment during their operations in Vietnam. In 1968 alone, the 1st Air Cavalry lost twenty helicopters due to rain and saw numerous operations postponed or negatively impacted. One such was Operation Delaware, an effort to use air power to clear the A Shau Valley. Tolson, in his study on air mobility during Vietnam, identified that while the military had learned to consider the aspect of rain in its relationship to the undertaking of an operation, it focused too heavily on weather and not climate. "An inch of rain that falls in thirty minutes is not nearly as important as a tenth of an inch which falls as a light mist over 24 hours."[90] The North Vietnamese understood the value of airpower to the American strategy and sought to neutralize it using both terrain and weather. The Easter

Offensive launched by the North in 1972 was specifically organized around the onset of the monsoon season, which hampered American air operations for months.

A decade later similar conditions plagued the initial American assault on the tiny island of Grenada. Rain squalls delayed the landing of several units by helicopter and impacted combat throughout the campaign. During the initial insertion of Special Forces, a storm caused a transport plane to ditch at sea. Four Navy SEALs were lost in the ocean, 20 percent of the battle's overall casualties.

Rain proved to be an influential component in military operations for thousands of years. This was due to both its impact on movement as well as its role in serving as a catalyst for disease. While the latter element has largely been neutralized with the advent of modern medicine, bacteriology, and technology, rain can still have a debilitating effect on movement. Even in the heart of industrialized nations with modern transportation technology, heavy storms and flooding can still wreak havoc on armies. Finally, success or failure in war still comes down to the presence of the foot soldier and his ability to move and fight on the battlefield. Heavy rains do not only hamper these but can also seriously affect troop morale as well.

4

FOG

For the fog of war shrouds Hector and cloaks our doom.
Call now to the Greek generals, if there are any to hear.
—Homer, *Iliad*, Book XVII

Clausewitz's famous aphorism about the "fog of war," while specifically dealing with political and military planning, is just as accurate when relating to weather. While rain hindered movement and spread disease, fog affected the sight of a commander and his troops, disguising movement and making, "things seem grotesque and larger than they really are."[91] In addition, unlike rain, fog tends to restrict itself to certain regions and areas and even becomes predictable to the local population in many cases. Throughout history generals who have learned to utilize it have been able to apply it as a force multiplier in combat, moving troops unexpectedly and disguising their position. In this sense, fog serves to expand the element of darkness in war, and produces many of the same consequences.

One of the earliest mentions of fog in combat comes from ancient Chinese mythology. During the legendary fight for the control of the Yellow River region between the Yellow Emperor and Chi You, the latter used his mystical powers to summon fog onto the battlefield. The soldiers under the command of the Yellow Emperor became confused and lost, threatening to hand victory over to Chi You. According to legend, the Yellow Emperor created a South-Pointing Chariot, a magnetic or mechanical instrument that allowed his men to maneuver through the mist and find and defeat the army of Chi You.

Such an invention would have been useful to the Macedonians at the Battle of Cynoscephalae in 197 BC. A heavy fog blanketing the hills between the Roman forces and those of King Philip led to the Macedonian phalanxes being hindered from proper deployment. Victory went to Titus Flamininus, and the myth of the Greek phalanx's invincibility as a weapons system began to crumble. Although the ability of the individual Roman soldier and the advantage of their formation cannot be discounted, weather also played a significant part in choosing the legion as the model for combat for the next six hundred years.

The Bible mentions the presence of a fog during the flight of the Jews from Egypt. According to the book of Exodus, God led Moses and his people in the form of a pillar of cloud by day and one of fire by night as they moved across the desert toward the Red Sea. Far from being simply a means of direction however, the phenomenon also served to hinder the pursuing Egyptian army. "And the Angel of God, who went before the camp of Israel, moved and went behind them; and the pillar of cloud went from before them and stood behind them. So it came between the camp of the Egyptians and the camp of Israel. Thus it was a cloud and darkness to the one, and it gave light by night to the other, so that the one did not come near the other all that night."[92] By obfuscating the sight of the Pharaoh's pursuing chariots, the Jews were able to cross the Red Sea and extract themselves from Egypt. The importance of this weather-related event for the Jews is evident from its adoption as an operational nomenclature during a 2012 Israeli campaign in the Gaza Strip.

Almost twenty-five hundred years later, fog helped to secure the throne of England for Edward IV. A month after the Yorkist army under Edward had landed in England, it engaged a Lancastrian army under the Earl of Warwick at the Battle of Barnet in April of 1471. During the preceding night, Edward had executed a clandestine maneuver by moving his army toward the Lancastrian position in order to launch a surprise morning assault. However, both sides awoke to a heavy fog hanging over the battlefield. According to local lore, the famed magician Friar Bungay had conjured up the mist in order to aid the House of York.[93] Unbeknownst to either side, their right wings vastly overestimated the position of the opposing line, leading to both hanging off of the battlefield. John de Vere, the Earl of Oxford, took advantage of this first, outflanking and defeating his opposite number. Yet, the fog would then turn against Oxford, turning his prospective victory into ultimate defeat. Much later, as his men returned from chasing the fleeing Yorkists, Oxford became disoriented in the fog and attacked his ally Montagu's troops by mistake. In the confusion that followed, chaos erupted in the center of the Lancastrian line, allowing Edward to commit his reserves and achieve victory. A number of enemy lords, including Warwick and Montagu, were killed, a loss that would prove to be as devastating for the cause of Henry VI as the loss of the battle itself.

A similar case of mistaken deployment due to foggy conditions occurred at the Battle of Zutphen in the Netherlands in 1586. The Earl of Leicester was attempting to blockade and besiege the Spanish garrison town of Zutphen when he was apprised of an approaching enemy supply convoy. The English decided to ambush the Spanish force, but due to a particularly heavy fog they positioned themselves too close to the approaching enemy and were themselves surprised. The Spanish went on to win the battle, resupplying the town and severely damaging the Anglo-Dutch war effort. In fact, the action helped to lead to the downfall of Leicester and the appointment of Count Maurice of Nassau who would soon rise to fame in Dutch history. The heavy fog also helped to lead to the death of Sir Philip Sidney, whose demise at the battle would lead to his subsequent apotheosis in Elizabethan England.

Forty-six years later, King Gustavus Adolphus of Sweden met a similar fate at the Battle of Lutzen. In order to halt the successful

Imperial campaign in central Germany, the Swedish king launched an unexpected late-fall attack against the army of Albrecht von Wallenstein. As the latter had recently split his forces, Adolphus felt confident that a quick and certain attack would throw the forces of the Catholic League off-balance before the onset of winter. Unfortunately for him, a dense fog delayed the deployment of Swedish troops, giving Count Pappenheim time to return with his cavalry reinforcements. Likewise, a charge by Gustavus Adolphus soon became disoriented due to the combination of the fog and the smoke from the battle. The King, cut off and isolated, was subsequently killed in action. Though at the end of the day the Swedes could claim victory, the cost was enormous, and the death of Gustavus would have a lasting impact both at home and abroad. A century later, Wellington's second-in-command, Edward Paget, was captured in Spain after blundering into a French patrol in the fog; an embarrassment for the British government.

Fog often served to allow men to move unnoticed by the enemy outside of battle, bringing needed reinforcements or supplies to surrounded armies and besieged cities. An example of this includes the arrival of a column of Spanish troops to reinforce the besieged Knights at Malta in 1565. In late June of that year, after a month of attacks, Ottoman forces had slowly advanced over the islands and had recently captured Fort St. Elmo. The unseasonal arrival of the Sirocco winds from North Africa brought a dense, white fog to Malta and allowed Melchior de Robles to move seven hundred fresh reserves across the Kalkara Creek and into the fortress of the Knights. In 1708, the Duke of Marlborough was similarly able to move his army across the Scheldt River under the guns of the opposing French army, thanks to the arrival of a timely fog.

Just as frequently, fog could give an advantage to an attacking force, helping to make up for lesser numbers or serve to reduce casualties. This was precisely the case at the capture of Dumbarton Castle in April of 1571 where a small band of men under Thomas Crawford scaled the rocky cliffs under the cover of mist. Sir David Leslie's Covenanter attack on the Royalist forces of Montrose at Philiphaugh in 1645 enjoyed a similar boost as well. At the latter event, Montrose mistakenly encamped his men in a low-lying area, which became enshrouded in fog the next morning. Leslie was able to ride into the camp largely unnoticed and routed the Royalist army. The engagement served to end King Charles I's ambitions in Scotland. Archduke Charles of Austria would also utilize fog to help his men bridge the defenses of Mannheim and take that fortress in 1799. Finally, the English fleet under John Leake used fog to approach and defeat a French fleet at Cabrita Point in 1705, helping to end the Franco-Spanish siege of Gibraltar.

Not unsurprisingly, fog proved to be a reoccurring motif in naval warfare. During the War of Spanish Succession, a richly laden English merchant fleet sailing from the Near East managed to elude a French squadron in the Bay of Tunis, thanks to a timely dense fog. In 1743 during a war with Russia, a Swedish fleet managed to extradite itself from Hango under similar circumstances. Finally, a year later in 1744, the returning Lord Anson was able to bring his treasure-filled ship *Centurion* into Portsmouth thanks to a fog which hid him from patrolling French ships. Yet, the British Royal Navy was not always so lucky, as the HMS *Venerable* became lost in a heavy fog in November of 1804 and was wrecked on the rocks near Torbay, England while the HMS *Tiger* suffered a similar fate in 1854 at Odessa. Other countries suffered similar misfortunes. While hoping to use fog to take Anholt in 1811, a Danish fleet found itself surprised instead by a larger British opponent.

Some of the greatest generals and rulers met their matches in the unpredictable fog of war, perhaps none more often than Frederick the Great of Prussia. At the end of August in 1756, Frederick launched an invasion of Saxony as part of the Seven Years' War. After a month of successful campaigning, his army approached Lobositz in Bohemia. A larger Austrian force under Maximilian Ulysses von Browne concealed itself in a dense fog and surprised the unsuspecting Prussians. After several hours of brutal fighting, both sides disengaged, and though Frederick would attempt to proclaim victory, in actuality he had been badly mauled in his first major campaign of the war. Two years later, the Austrians again used the cover of fog to markedly defeat the German king. Early on the morning of October 14, 1758, Marshal Leopold Josef Graf Daun launched an attack using small units against the Prussian army at Hochkirch. At the end of the day Frederick was forced to withdraw, having lost over a quarter of his army.

The Duke of Marlborough was not the only commander who used fog to extradite an army from a difficult situation. George Washington achieved most of his fame as a military commander due to his ability to preserve the fledgling American army by strong leadership, ingenious subterfuge, and timely withdrawals. Perhaps his most famous retreat followed the disastrous Battle of Long Island in 1776. After being decisively defeated by General Howe, Washington was faced with the prospect of being trapped between the British Army and Royal Navy and therefore decided to withdraw his army under cover of darkness to Manhattan. The process of moving the soldiers, wounded men, and material took longer than expected and as the sun rose it looked as if Washington and his covering force under Thomas Mifflin would be captured. Luckily for the Americans, "Providence interposed in favor of the retreating army."[94] At some point during the late night or early morning hours of August 29–30, a heavy fog descended over Long Island. Though the majority of the American army appears to have already been moved by the time the weather turned, thus disputing apocryphal claims that Washington had used the fog to withdraw his men, the fog did allow the General and his covering force to retreat as well as secure all of the army's equipment, which were equally important maneuvers. Washington would go on to conduct his famed march through New Jersey culminating in the American attack at Trenton in late December.

Yet, fog was not always so kind to General Washington and the American cause. A year after his withdrawal from Brooklyn, the American commander in chief was positioning his troops at the various fords of the Brandywine Creek. Unbeknownst to him the British had identified another crossing point farther to the north and set out to outflank the American line. In this, Howe was aided by the rise of a dense fog that blanketed the river and hid his advance from Washington's scouts. The American general, believing that the main attack was still coming from the south, reacted too slowly, and by the end of the day the British were victorious. Two weeks later the British entered the new nation's capital.

The French suffered an equally disastrous reverse at Wurzburg in September of 1796. General Jean-Baptiste Jourdan and his revolutionary French army advanced through southern Germany toward the Main River. Finding an isolated Austrian unit, Jourdan formed his men for battle and advanced against the enemy. Unfortunately for him a heavy fog blanketed the battlefield, hiding the true size of the Austrian army and covering their continuing efforts to cross the river. Jourdan was ultimately defeated and soon after Moreau's forces were also driven from Germany. General Francois Marceau used the heavy fog to escape from encirclement by a superior Austrian force after the subsequent Battle of Limburg. Though he managed to extradite his army, he himself was mortally wounded while falling back to Altenkirchen. Only the successful campaign of Napoleon Bonaparte in Italy around the same time gave hope to the French cause.

As is usual in military literature, the successful use of fog by other contemporary generals such as Archduke Charles at Mannheim and Moreau at Limburg has been overshadowed in historical literature by the more renowned actions of Napoleon. One of the most famous battles of the latter, that of Austerlitz in December of 1805, hinged almost entirely on a dense morning mist. Outnumbered and facing an enemy on higher ground, Napoleon planned on a daring assault on the center of the Austro-Russian army. Luckily for the French emperor a heavy fog blanketed the chilly battlefield, hiding the movement of St. Hilaire's men. The phenomenon was critical enough to catch the attention of Leo Tolstoy who included it in his seminal work, *War and Peace*. French historian Georges Blond would likewise later refer to it as, "a precious ally."[95] As the French climbed the slope the "sun of Austerlitz" suddenly broke through the sky, revealing to the assembled Russian army the assaulting troops of Napoleon. By the end of the day not only was the Austro-Russian army broken, but Napoleon had established himself as the master of a continent.

A year later, Napoleon would again use fog to position his army closer to enemy lines, this time defeating the Duke of Brunswick and his Prussian army at Jena and Auerstedt. In 1808 a Polish cavalry charge took the Pass at Somosierra thanks to a heavy morning mist that otherwise would have produced horrific casualties. Finally, Marshal Soult used the same tactic to assault General Rowland Hill's lines at St. Pierre in 1813 near the end of the Peninsular War.

One of the engagements in world history most associated with fog is the Battle of Inkerman during the Crimean War. Inspired no doubt by Napoleon, Prince Menshikov hoped to utilize the cover of fog to advance his Russian army from the soon-to-be-besieged city of Sevastopol, toward the British and French lines across the Tchernaya River. While the Russians did experience some local success thanks to the blanketing of the field, the fog in this case affected the ability of units to accurately coordinate. The battle has been called by many historians "the Soldier's Battle," due to the requirement of many units to fight on the level of a battalion or smaller, due to the overwhelming fog. Small-unit combat, a hallmark of much later wars, became a necessity in this one as a result of the weather.

The American Civil War also featured several battles that were impacted by the presence of fog. Most notable among these was the so-called "Battle Above the Clouds" at Lookout Mountain in November of 1863. The hilltop is known for a weather phenomenon that occurs from three to five times a year, in which an extraordinarily heavy cloud of fog forms at the bottom of the mountain, on occasion even shrouding the entire peak. Though locals would have been familiar with the occurrence, and some of Hooker's troops and commanders were from the area, it is unknown whether he incorporated it into his planning.

The dense mist allowed General John Geary to move his men up the mountain and kept Confederate artillery from effectively engaging the Union soldiers. By the end of the day the battle had been won, Chattanooga was saved from Confederate investment, and the road was open for Sherman's subsequent Atlanta Campaign.

The advent of the twentieth century saw advancements in technology that could often mitigate the effect of such weather conditions as fog. At the Battle of Tsushima during the Russo-Japanese War, a heavy fog separated the two fleets in the Korea Strait. In his after-battle action report, Admiral Togo recounted that, "Thus, though a heavy fog covered the sea, making it impossible to observe anything at a distance of over five miles, all the conditions of the enemy were as clear to us, who were thirty or forty miles distant, as though they had been under our very eyes." The reason for this was that the Japanese had spotted several Russian hospital ships which had stayed illuminated in the heavy fog. Using wireless communication, Admiral Togo was able to coordinate his forces for an attack on the enemy. The vast majority of the Russian fleet was sunk to the bottom of the Strait with over forty-three hundred killed. With proper technology, even the fog of war could be penetrated. Thus by the time of the invasion of Normandy in 1944, though fog interfered with sailing and airdrops, it did not significantly hinder the success of the operation.

Yet failure to use or understand technology could still result in catastrophe. The same Russian fleet that was later sunk at the Tsushima Strait, as it was departing the North Sea in 1904 came upon a group of British fishing boats at Dogger Bank. A heavy fog blanketed the sea and Admiral Rozhestvensky ordered his ships to open fire on what he perceived to be Japanese torpedo boats. In the tragedy that followed, several Englishmen were killed before the Russian fleet moved on. The Dogger Bank Incident, as it became known, brought the two nations close to war, a situation made more tenuous by an active alliance between the United Kingdom and the Japanese Empire.

Fog remained a factor on the battlefield in World War I as well, and early on helped to aid the German advance during the Spring Offensive of 1918. Operation Michael was organized by the German High Command to serve as a last attempt to split the Allied lines and bring a close to the war before the arrival of American units on the battlefield in large numbers. Violent rainstorms preceded the opening of battle, which Hindenburg hoped "would probably shroud our final preparations."[96] The German attackers awoke to heavy fog shrouding the field through which their artillery fired blindly and their men advanced with trepidation. Though the initial attack by the Germans largely succeeded in pushing back the English, time, lack of ammunition, and numbers proved to be against the Germans and the entire offensive soon became mired down.

With the advent of airpower, the issue of fog on land was matched in the air by cloud cover. The initial date for the invasion of Normandy had to be pushed back as dense cloud cover obscured German troop movements and potential sea swells threatened both landing craft and Mulberry harbors. Likewise, American troops trapped at the Bulge in December of 1944 were without air support as the 9th Air Force was grounded by snow and cloud cover. Hitler had largely organized this last, desperate campaign around the harsh weather patterns that blanketed the Ardennes region in early winter. Though the fog that blanketed the hills and forest initially helped to disguise the movement of German units, the American soldiers were soon able to likewise use it to sneak bazooka teams through the forest to damage and disable the various panzer units.[97] The anticipated fog also proved to be fickle, lifting early at some points and severely limiting the initial German thrust.

In the Pacific, Japanese forces were initially unsuccessful in their bombing raid on Dutch Harbor in 1942 due to heavy fog, while the onset of more severe weather soon afterward led to the cancellation of the invasion of Adak Island. Overcast skies even went so far as to alter the planned atomic bombing of Japan. After the bombing of

Hiroshima, the second American nuclear attack was planned for the city of Kokura in northern Kyushu. Luckily for the residents of that city, dense cloud cover and lingering smoke from the previous day's firebombing of nearby Yawata left the target too obscured for a visual drop. The American bomber carrying the second atomic weapon therefore diverted to the backup target of Nagasaki.

Vietnam, with its monsoon climate, frequently saw operations impacted by storms and fog. Operation Masher, a massive search-and-destroy mission launched in Binh Dinh Province in 1966, was so delayed by fog in the low-lying valley regions that a weather unit had to be flown in by helicopter to help plan around the conditions. Heavy fog also hindered American efforts to support the Marines at Khe Sanh in 1968, much as it had at the Bulge a generation before. Though Northern antiaircraft crews were also reduced to firing blindly into the clouds, the sounds of the planes and helicopters at least aided in their efforts. A combination of desperation and ingenuity led Westmoreland to order the dropping of salt over the area in an attempt to break up the fog and allow for resupply by air. Learning from its experiences, the NVA rolled its tanks over the Southern border in 1972 under the cover of a heavy monsoonal fog as well.

Fog continues to be a factor in war, especially in low-level conflicts that still focus on small-unit engagements. Most recently during the Kurdish Tel Abyad Offensive in 2015, Islamic State fighters often utilized the cover of fog in the region to launch attacks.[98] Even the most modern of militaries are not exempted from its affects. In the late 1990s during the Kosovo War, NATO reported having to cancel almost half of its bombing missions during the first two weeks of the operation due to covering fog.[99]

From the Bible to the modern battlefield, fog has remained a factor in the waging of war. While lacking the disease-related component of rain, it has both hampered and saved armies. Likewise, in our modern era of aerial warfare, clouds and fog can do much to reduce the technological advantages of a great power. Unlike rain, it also is a weather phenomenon that can be simulated by man. As will be seen in a subsequent chapter, the use of obscuring smoke has a long history in human conflict, no doubt influenced in part by experiences with fog.

5

WIND

Flavit et Dissipati Sunt.
(He blew, and they were scattered.)
—Medallion commemorating the defeat of the
Spanish Armada

Wind represents a powerful but often geographically limited factor in the history of warfare. While many campaigns on land have been altered by powerful or unexpected windstorms, the greatest instances have tended to naturally occur at sea or along coastal settlements. Hurricanes, typhoons, cyclones, and destructive storms at sea have all impacted not only human settlement and history, but naval warfare and land-based combat as well. In comparison to rain, fog, or snow, this type of weather is unmatched for its inherent destructiveness and potential to cause massive loss of life. Historically, regions living in such conditions have learned to time these events and plan accordingly. More often than not, nations who have fallen victim to such storms did so due to a failure to appreciate local conditions and weather patterns.

Heavy wind as a metaphor for the voice or power of a god is a classical literary device. Nowhere is this more pronounced than in the famous story of the Hebrews' escape from Egypt in the Old Testament. According to the book of Exodus, "Then Moses stretched out his hand over the sea; and the LORD swept the sea back by a strong east wind all night and turned the sea into dry land, so the waters were divided. The sons of Israel went through the midst of the sea on the dry land, and the waters were like a wall to them on their right hand and on their left."[100] By means of an obviously powerful wind, the Red Sea was separated, allowing the Hebrews to cross the body of water. As the chariots of the Egyptian army followed the wind died, washing away the pharaoh's army.

While the episode is often treated historically as an allegory or poetic exaggeration, similar situations have occurred at other times in military history. From 1711 to 1715 an allied army from Russia, Prussia, Denmark, and Saxony besieged the Swedish fortress at Stralsund on the Baltic Sea. Yet, the defenses of the town proved to be too difficult to overcome directly and the campaign dragged on for several years. Thanks to a defecting Swedish soldier, however, the allies discovered a peculiar weather pattern in the area. As recounted later by Voltaire . . .

> No one had remarked before that in a strong westerly wind the waves of the Baltic roll back so as to leave only three feet of water under the entrenchment. They had always thought it deep. A soldier, happening to fall from the top of the entrenchment, was surprised to find a bottom; but having made that discovery, he concluded that it might make his fortune.[101]

The besieging soldiers were able to ford the water they previously believed to be impregnable, to directly assault the Swedish walls. Stralsund fell to the allies and Sweden went on to lose the Great Northern War.

The Russians would repeat the tactic a generation later in 1737. The year prior, Field Marshal Burkhard von Münnich stormed the Tartar fortress of Perekop in the Crimea. Despite his brilliant success in opening up the Crimean Peninsula, disease and lack of supplies forced his withdrawal shortly afterward. The Tartars then quickly reoccupied and refortified the isthmus, reversing Russian gains. In

1737 another Russian army, this one under Count Peter Lacy, discovered that under certain wind conditions the Sivash Bay was actually fordable. Lacy used this knowledge to launch a surprise assault which took Perekop and opened the way to a general Russian invasion of the Crimean Peninsula over the next few years, finally securing for Catherine the Great her much-desired warmwater port. Soviet forces would repeat the crossing almost two centuries later during the Russian Civil War.

Nor were the early Hebrews the only people who saw the impact of wind on an enemy as a sign of divine providence. A massive storm at sea served the role of a plot element in Homer's *Odyssey*, bringing divine retribution to the returning Greek fleet following its sack of Troy. Thus, when confronted by the overwhelming power of the Persian army and navy several centuries later, the Greeks sought to employ the same gods to ensure victory. During Darius's first invasion of Greece in 492 BC, Herodotus recorded that, "a great and irresistible north wind fell upon them as they sailed past and dealt very roughly with them."[102] The Greeks claimed that the wind disabled or destroyed three hundred enemy ships and drowned more than twenty thousand men.

The subsequent Persian invasions of the Hellenic world in 490 BC and 480 BC were also substantially impacted by the stormy weather and winds of the Aegean Sea. Despite the Athenian victory at Marathon, the enemy commander Datis decided to sail south and attack Athens directly. This strategy may suggest that Marathon itself was simply a minor action meant to draw the main Greek army away from the city, allowing the Persian navy to then outpace and assault a poorly defended Athens. At this moment it seems that the winds turned against the Greeks. The Aegean is dominated by the Etesian wind current from June to September, which pushes south toward Attica, propelling any sailing ship in the water at high speeds toward Cape Sounion. In fact, the Persian fleet seems to have remained at Marathon for several days, perhaps waiting for the right wind conditions to quickly send them south in order to reach Athens before the Athenian soldiers. As the vast majority of ships and sailors in Datis's fleet would have been from Asia Minor or Phoenicia, it is reasonable to assume that there was some knowledge of this weather pattern. Unfortunately for Darius, the Athenians were also able to quickly return to their city, and the late-arriving Spartan army only further steeled Greek resistance. A combination of poor wind conditions and an overreliance on favorable ones doomed the Persian invasion.

Philip II of Macedonia would later use the same Etesian Winds to aid his campaigns in the Chalcidice. In 357 BC, Philip began to besiege the important city of Amphipolis, a town which Athens formerly held claim to on the northern coast of the Aegean Sea. In order to mask his ambitions, Philip announced that he intended to return the prize to Athens once he conquered it. The largest obstacle to Greek intervention were the Etesian Winds. The Macedonian ruler carefully timed his actions against the city to coincide with the winds, thus preventing Athenian naval units from sailing north.[103] Philip repeated his tactic several years later in 348 BC at the Siege of Olynthos, as once again the Athenians were unable to halt his expansion.

While wind briefly impacted the First Persian Invasion, it heavily molded Xerxes's invasion a decade later. According to Herodotus, as the Persian army and fleet once more approached Greece, "the men of Delphi consulted the Oracle of the god on behalf of themselves and on behalf of Hellas, being struck with dread; and a reply was given them that they should pray to the Winds, for these would be powerful helpers of Hellas in fight."[104] The Athenians would credit their prayers to Boreas, the god of the north wind, as the reason behind the wrecking of much of the Persian fleet off of Magnesia.[105] In a more practical manifestation, Eurybiades used his knowledge of the local wind conditions to subsequently deliver a crushing blow to the remaining Persian ships at the Battle of Artemisium shortly afterward. Themistocles followed a similar strategy afterward at Salamis. Knowing the wind conditions in the Saronic Gulf, the Athenian commander planned to draw the Persian navy deep into the channel until the onset of the local wind would prevent them from retreating or maneuvering:

> There regularly blows in a fresh breeze from the open sea, and brings in with it a strong swell into the channel; which was no inconvenience to the Greek ships, which were low-built, and little above the water, but did much hurt to the Persians, which had high sterns and lofty decks, and were heavy and cumbrous in their movements.[106]

The resulting battle proved to be a tremendous victory for the Greeks, ending the Persian hopes of expanding into Europe.

Stormy seas, however, likewise dashed Athens's own hopes for empire. In the climate of political chaos that followed the Theban War, Athens made an attempt to once again expand its influence and power in the Hellenic world. Resentment and resistance toward this policy erupted into the Social War of 357–355 BC. The Athenian loss in this was hinged in part upon various storms at sea that weakened or destroyed their ships. In the first year of the conflict, the Athenian general, Chares, sailed into the Hellespont unsupported by his other commanders as they feared the stormy weather that had suddenly descended upon them. Thus reduced in strength, his fleet was defeated by the navies of Chios and Byzantium. A year later a similar situation unfolded at the Battle of Embata in which two-thirds of the Athenian fleet was kept away by windy weather leaving Chares too weak to defeat the enemy. Athens was eventually forced to come to terms, granting independence to many of its former possessions and giving Persia dominance once more in Asia Minor.

The western Mediterranean Sea, with its own maritime kingdoms and its own unique weather patterns, also experienced a number of wind- and storm-influenced battles in the ancient world. Traditionally, on the same day that Themistocles was employing his knowledge of local winds to stop the Persian fleet at Salamis, a similar situation unfolded at Himera in Sicily. A large Carthaginian fleet was sailing across the Mediterranean Sea to attack the forces of Syracuse when it was suddenly struck by adverse winds and storm:

> Now as he was crossing the Libyan sea he encountered a storm and lost the vessels which were carrying the horses and chariots. And when he came to port in Sicily in the harbour of Panormus he remarked that he had finished the war; for he had been afraid that the sea would rescue the Siceliotes from the perils of the conflict.[107]

The loss of men and ships, and especially that of his cavalry and chariots, would severely impact Hamilcar's performance at the subsequent Battle of Himera. The Carthaginian disaster would preserve Greek independence in Sicily for the next seventy years.

Wind and rain continued to be a problem for campaigns in the region following the arrival of the Romans. The First Punic War, which erupted in 264 BC, mirrored the early Peloponnesian War in that while the Romans focused on their land-based army, the Carthaginians were dominant at sea. Polybius credited much of the eventual Roman victory to a chance storm at sea around 260 BC. At some point that year a Carthaginian ship foundered in heavy winds off of the coast of Sicily. Locals recovered the wreck and the Romans were able to design and build their own ships accordingly.[108] Thanks in large part to this chance occurrence, the Romans were able to subsequently defeat a Carthaginian fleet at Mylae. Wind, like all other weather patterns however, does not differentiate between friend and foe, and the Romans themselves lost two fleets in heavy winds off of Sicily at Pachynus and Palinurus during the 250s. A Roman rescue fleet dispatched after the disaster at Bagradas did successfully embark much of the remaining Latin army, but its subsequent destruction at sea by a storm permanently ended all hope of renewed Roman raids on Africa. The final battle of the war, fought at the Aegates Islands in 241 BC, occurred in very windy conditions. Prepared for this, Gaius Catulus had removed the masts and much of the equipment from his ships, thus making them less susceptible to sinking. Likewise, the experienced Roman crew was better able to handle the windy and choppy conditions than the freshly drafted Carthaginian sailors. The victory not only ended the First Punic War, but also secured Sicily for the Roman Republic.

Similar storms would reappear during the Second Punic War, helping to mitigate the overall Carthaginian strategy and success of Hannibal. A planned surprise assault by the Punic navy on Sicily was foiled in 218 BC when a portion of the fleet was blown off course and captured by ships from Syracuse. Alerted, the Romans were able to prepare a fleet under Marcus Amellius and defeat the Carthaginians at Lilybaeum. Likewise, the Carthaginians launched another expedition several years later in 215 BC to aid an uprising in Sardinia. Contrary winds pushed the Carthaginians back to the Balearic Islands, thus giving the Romans time to reinforce the local garrison and defeat the rebels at the Battle of Cornus. Thanks to these instances of foul weather, the Roman Republic was saved from multiple invasions and could more efficiently focus on Hannibal's campaign in the peninsula.

Both the rise and spread of Christianity and Islam were also impacted by the actions of wind. Following the mysterious death of the Western Roman Emperor Valentinian II in 392 AD, the Frankish general Arbogast placed the pro-pagan Flavius Eugenius on the throne. Christianity had only a tenuous hold on the western half of the Roman world, with the vast majority of the Senate and landed elite openly hostile to it. In response, Emperor Theodosius I, who ruled over the eastern half of the empire, declared his own son's candidacy for the throne and marched west toward Rome. The two forces met at the Battle of the Frigidus near the modern-day border between Italy and Slovenia. The first day of battle ended in favor of the Western troops, with Theodosius's men being badly mauled in a frontal assault. Suddenly on the second day, a local wind phenomenon known as a bora drove down from the mountains, buffeting the Western Roman army, throwing up considerable dust, and deflecting their arrows. As recounted later by Ambrose of Milan, "So the army of non-believers deserved to be struck blind."[109] Theodosius seized upon the moment by throwing his lines forward and defeating the army of Arbogast and Eugenius. Considerable debate still exists as to the exact existential threat that Eugenius's rise to power posed to Christianity in the West. Yet, the portrayal of the battle by Theodosius, Ambrose, and others came to be accepted as the truth, thus elevating the role of the bora wind to a divine phenomenon.

Nearly three centuries later, the prophet Muhammed was beginning to launch small raids from Medina against the Quraysh tribe in Mecca. These attacks culminated in the pivotal Battle of Badr in 624. Mohammed had sent a large force of around three hundred men to raid a wealthy caravan en route to Mecca. Unfortunately, the Quraysh had either anticipated this move or else had received intelligence of his design and had organized a force of a thousand cavalry to trap and defeat the opposing force at the Badr Oasis. Though seemingly trapped and outnumbered, the Muslims fought back ferociously, and according to the Quran, it was not the skill of the men but the power of Allah that saved them: "And you did not kill them, but it was Allah who killed them. And you threw not, O Mohammed, when you threw [the dust], but it was Allah who threw that He might test the believers with a good test."[110] A series of thunderstorms that had passed through the area the night before apparently created a giant wind-driven dust storm known as a haboob. A wall of dust slammed into the Meccan army, hindering their ability to fight and delivering victory to Mohammed.

The mystery and power of the wind, especially necessary for campaigns at sea, continued to inspire divine appeals for centuries. In August of 1066, as William the Conqueror of Normandy readied his invasion force in order to claim the throne of England, a calm set in and confined his fleet to the mouth of the Dives River. When he finally did sail several weeks later the winds proved to be too strong and he was forced back to St. Valery. According to tradition, William had the relics of St. Valery himself brought out and prayers said for a fortnight at which point the winds suddenly shifted and allowed for him to depart for England and the subsequent Battle of Hastings. Whether his delay was intentional or not, it proved to be rather fortuitous for the Normans. King Harold had been forced to relocate his forces to the north in the meantime to battle a Norwegian invasion by Harald Haldrada, thus allowing William to land unopposed when the winds finally favored him. William's son, King William II, would be similarly delayed, but in the opposite direction, in 1094 attempting to launch a fleet from Hastings to defeat a rebellion in Normandy.

Other members of the Plantagenet family seem to have also suffered severe reverses due to the impact of wind, especially when sailing far afield to fight in the Crusades. Notable among these was King Richard the Lionheart who nearly lost his throne and his life to a strong gust of wind. In 1192, while sailing home from the Third Crusade, the English monarch's ship was twice pushed ashore by winds and rain until he was ultimately forced to ride with only a handful of attendants overland to return home. In December, he was captured near Vienna by Duke Leopold V of Austria and confined to jail for a number of political and criminal reasons. It would be over a year before he was released and returned to England, during which time his brother John had attempted to seize the throne. Finally, less than a century later in 1271, Edward I found himself fighting the Ninth Crusade largely alone as heavy winds had pushed back the fleets of Charles of Anjou and Philip III.

One of the greatest incidents involving an invasion being stopped by wind remains the two failed Mongolian attempts to conquer Japan during the thirteenth century. After taking the islands of Tsushima and Iki and slaughtering their inhabitants, the Mongols landed their main army on Kyushu Island. After being temporarily stopped by the Japanese, the Mongol commander ordered his men to return to their ships for the night. A late-season typhoon abruptly descended upon the invasion fleet, sinking hundreds of ships and hiding the approach of smaller Japanese craft, which were subsequently able to swarm the remaining vessels. Divine winds (*kamikaze*) had saved the Japanese islands from the fate of the rest of Asia.

Not to be deterred, Kublai Khan launched a second, much larger invasion in 1281. Once again the Mongols would be landing in the midst of typhoon season, which traditionally lasted from July to September. A number of Japanese victories combined with hastily constructed defensive works kept the Mongols aboard their ships deep into August. A massive typhoon then struck the area, sinking boats and killing thousands. The occurrence of two typhoons, which served to save the Japanese homeland, resulted in their elevation to divine status. The Japanese would forever consider their islands to be protected by divine winds, a belief that would have disastrous consequences in World War II.

Around the same time, a Norwegian attempt to reassert its control over Scotland was likewise deterred by fierce winds at sea. In 1262, King Haakon IV of Norway sent an expedition west to secure the Hebrides and Orkneys. By the beginning of fall in 1263, the invading fleet was anchored in the Firth of Clyde awaiting the outcome of negotiations. One night at the end of September, a powerful storm broke out and ravaged the Norwegian fleet. High winds forced a number of boats ashore and scattered most of the rest. Over the next several days while Haakon attempted to rescue his men and refloat his ships, a Scottish army under Alexander Stewart, the High Steward of Scotland, arrived in the area. The resulting Battle of Largs, though largely inconclusive, ended with the Norwegians withdrawing to the Hebrides where Haakon would subsequently die. The war would soon come to a close, ending several centuries of Viking control in Scotland.

Much as rainy weather impacted the use of certain forms of technology, so too did heavy winds. The reliance on archery from ancient times to the adoption of firearms in the late Middle Ages provide ample opportunities for wind to play a role in shaping the course of battle. This was certainly the case at the Battle of Towton in 1461 at the height of the Wars of the Roses. Heavy headwinds caused the Lancastrian archers to shoot their arrows in vain, inflicting no damage on the Yorkist archers who simply stood their ground waiting. Once the harmless barrage ceased, the Yorkists stepped forward and loosed their arrows, aided by the wind, and devastated the Lancastrian front ranks. Once battle was joined, the charging Lancastrians found their movement hampered by their own arrows, which had fallen short and now littered the battlefield. The heavily outnumbered forces of Edward, the Duke of York, were able to obtain victory and compelled Henry VI to flee to France.

Several years later at the Battle of Barnet, which has already been mentioned due to the impact of fog on the battlefield, wind again helped to secure England for the House of York. Queen Margaret of Anjou and Edward, the Prince of Wales, had sailed from France on March 24, 1471, in order to deliver a southern blow against the Yorkist armies as Warwick moved south toward London. Storms and adverse winds would force the fleet back several times over the next three weeks, preventing a landing until the same day as the fighting at Barnet. Margaret and Edward had little choice but to proceed northwest toward Wales in hopes of joining with some remaining Lancastrian forces. Instead, the Yorkists met them at the Battle of Tewksbury on May 4, 1471, which resulted in a decisive victory for the house of York. Somerset, Devon, and Prince Edward all died while Queen Margaret was taken prisoner. The Yorkist faction would sit securely on the English throne for the next fourteen years.

The career of Joan of Arc hinged more upon a single episode of wind than almost anything else. Having appeared at the beginning of 1429 proclaiming that she was divinely appointed to secure victory for the French, Joan, after investigations by both royal and religious authorities, was brought to the besieged city of Orleans. Arguing for immediate action to be taken against the English, she was confronted by an understandably skeptical John of Dunois who informed her that he was more concerned about the adverse winds keeping his supplies from reaching the city than with her plans for an assault on the English positions. Then,

All of a sudden, and as though at that very moment, the wind—which had been contrary and which had absolutely prevented the ships in which were the food supplies for the city of Orleans from coming upriver—changed and became favorable. From that moment I had good hope in her, more than ever before.[111]

The arrival of supplies combined with the increased prestige of Joan to eventually help turn the tide of siege in favor of the French. The city was saved, the legend of the Maid of Orleans began, and the slow downfall of the English position in France commenced.

As the dominant naval force of the sixteenth century, the Spanish were often met with powerful storms at sea that could either help or hinder an expedition. A notable early example of this occurred in 1541 as Charles V sought to expand Habsburg control over the Mediterranean Coast. Heavy winds delayed the massive armada that he launched on Algiers for weeks. When the Spanish, Austrian, and Italian troops finally prepared to bombard and take the city, another storm suddenly struck, scattering the fleet, sinking dozens of ships, and killing hundreds of sailors. Turks and Berbers fell upon the unorganized soldiers struggling to land or save their comrades, slaughtering thousands. Charles V barely avoided capture and quickly sailed his battered force home.

Twenty-one years later, Charles V's successor, Philip II, assembled a fleet at Malaga to relieve the city of Oran in North Africa. The Ottomans were preparing to besiege the city and the Spanish monarch wished to head off the assault by dispatching twenty-eight galleys and some seven thousand men. Yet, only one day after setting sail, a massive storm hit the Alboran Sea. Don Juan Hurtado de Mendoza was forced to weather his ships in La Herradura Bay. Unfortunately, the storm changed direction the next morning, forcing the ships to crash into each other as they bobbed helplessly in the harbor. All but three of the galleys were sunk or beached and upwards of five thousand men perished.

The greatest disaster for the Spanish navy, however, remains the loss of the famed Spanish Armada in 1588. Thirty years before the English had found themselves unable to reinforce their territory in Calais due in part to adverse winds. Now, a large Spanish fleet was anchored in the same harbor preparing to bring aboard a seasoned army from the Spanish Netherlands for an invasion of England. The decision by the English to launch fireships toward the packed formation of the Spanish, while not inflicting damage, did manage to break up their formation, which a southwesterly wind prevented them from resuming. The English then closed for combat and managed to eke out a minor victory at Gravelines. Running short on supplies, fearing further attack, and beset by disease, the Duke of Medina Sidonia sailed northward toward Scotland to return to Spain around Ireland. A series of storms proceeded to wreck the Armanda off of the coast of Ireland. As most of the ships had abandoned their heavy anchors during the retreat from Gravelines, dozens of ships collided with one another. In the end, two-thirds of the Spanish Armada did not return home. King Philip himself is said to have exclaimed that, "I sent the Armada against men, not God's winds and waves." The Protestant Wind had saved England from invasion, secured Elizabeth on the throne, and ensured the continuation of the Reformation in that country.

In an eerie repetition of the Mongolian invasion attempts of Japan, subsequent Spanish naval campaigns against England suffered similar weather-related disasters. The Second Armada, which was launched in 1596, was initially delayed by early-autumn storms off of the coast of Spain. When it did sail, the fleet was almost immediately overtaken by storms and heavy winds off of Cape Finisterre. Almost a third of the Armada was sunk or damaged beyond repair, while another five thousand men were lost to either the ocean or disease.

Despite these losses and the third bankruptcy of Spain under Philip's reign, the Spanish pieced together yet another Armada to be launched the following year. This much larger, though more ill-prepared fleet, reached the English Channel by October of 1597. Yet, in a repetition of 1588, a massive storm lasting three days suddenly began to ravage the Armada. In the end, twenty-two Spanish ships would be destroyed and over a thousand men killed. The Armada was hopelessly dispersed and the lost time allowed the English to mount an active and effective defense of their coastline. Three Armadas had been effectively stopped more by the wind than by English gunnery, bringing an end to Spanish dominance in the Atlantic and ushering in an era of English exploration.

The Protestant Wind of 1588 would return a century later in 1688 during the Glorious Revolution. An adverse "Popish Wind" had already delayed William of Orange's crossing of the North Sea when suddenly it reversed in a favorable direction by late October. Yet the fleet was initially thrown back due to the return of a powerful wind from the northwest. About a week and a half after returning to the port of Hellevoetsluis, William once more set sail and by early November had entered the English Channel. Miraculously, the weather turned in his favor, as an initial fog and strong wind that had caused him to miss the port at Torbay suddenly lifted and reversed, allowing not only his men to land, but also bottling up the fleet of King James II under Dartmouth in Plymouth harbor. The English bishop Gilbert Burnet, who accompanied William of Orange, later recounted a line from the Latin poet Claudian: "Heaven's favorite for whom the skies do fight, and all the winds conspire to guide thee right."[112] Protestantism was twice saved in England by the power of wind.

Winds have stopped a number of other minor invasions and assaults as well. In 1627 an attempt by Admiral Charles Wilmot to relieve French Huguenot and English troops at La Rochelle was turned around due to gathering storms, leading to the defeat of the city soon afterward. Twenty-four years later, a naval expedition launched by Parliament during the English Civil War proved unable to land at the Isle of Man, though a local uprising soon turned the area over to Cromwell's control regardless. Edward Montagu, the 1st Earl of Sandwich, likewise saw an expedition against Algiers in 1661 ended due to storms.

William of Orange was not yet securely on the throne of England when the War of the League of Augsburg unfolded on the continent between France and a collection of other powers. Various battles in this Age of Sail continued to be frequently driven and influenced by the presence of wind. A French fleet under de Tourville managed a rare victory against the English navy at Beachy Head in 1690 due in part to Admiral Killgrew's squadron being delayed by wind in the Mediterranean. Two years later, the French admiral was again hindered from achieving victory, this time due to a heavy wind and the descent of fog on the English Channel at the Battle of Barfleur. Queen Mary seems to have fully understood the true cause of the English victory, writing that, "God alone delivered us." In 1694, an English fleet in the Mediterranean was struck by high winds while attempting to push through the Strait of Gibraltar. Two ships, the HMS *Cambridge* and HMS *Sussex* were sunk, and hundreds of men were drowned, including Sir Francis Wheeler, the commander of the expedition. A major attempt by Jacobite forces in 1708 under James Francis Edward Stuart, the Old Pretender, to invade Scotland and start a general uprising, was quelled by weather as well. A combination of measles and strong gales delayed and almost crippled Forbin's French navy. Though Stuart, "young as he was, faced the danger with a courage and coolness beyond his years; but his suite was thoroughly frightened."[113] In the end, Forbin called off the landing; England was once again secure.

The advent of colonial warfare between the great powers during the seventeenth and eighteenth centuries introduced new elements of wind into battle. The vast distances needed to be covered by the fleets of England and France meant that even minor adverse winds could produce an overall deleterious effect on an overseas campaign. Likewise, the spread of these wars to India and the Caribbean introduced new weather patterns and phenomena that European commanders had not previously had to contend with. An expedition launched by the English in 1711 to take Quebec was so delayed by ill winds crossing the Atlantic that it was ultimately aborted. Thirty-five years later the

French organized a fleet under the Duc d'Anville in order to recapture the fortress at Louisbourg. Adverse winds in the Bay of Biscay delayed the fleet to such an extent that disease soon began to ravage the crew. Further calms and lightning strikes cost more time and men as the French moved slowly across the Atlantic Ocean. Strong winds off of Sable Island so damaged the fleet that several warships had to return home. The largest pre-Revolution invasion force to be sent across the Atlantic ended up as a total failure, with little to show besides disease, death, and the loss of many ships. The Reverend Thomas Prince of Boston's call for God to, "Deliver us from our enemy! Send Thy tempest, Lord, upon the waters to the eastward! Raise Thy right hand. Scatter the ships of our tormentors and drive them hence. Sink their proud frigates beneath the power of Thy winds!" had been answered in full.[114] The British experienced the same tragedy in 1757 when Admiral Francis Holbourne's fleet was alternately struck by the combination of strong winds and a lack of winds while off of Halifax. Disease similarly decimated his crew and several ships ran aground when they were forced ashore. Similar fates befell Bertrand-François Mahé de La Bourdonnais, who, after taking Madras in 1746 lost much of his fleet to a cyclone in the Bay of Bengal, as well as the British raids on Cherbourg and St. Malo in 1758.

The next year, the decisive battle at sea in the Seven Years' War took place off of the coast of Brittany. Alfred Thayer Mahan would later refer to the Battle of Quiberon Bay as the Trafalgar of the Seven Years' War, a battle in which the wind fought on the side of the British.[115] A small French fleet of twenty-seven warships had used favorable winds to escape blockade at Brest. Followed closely by Sir Edward Hawke, the French under de Conflans turned to give battle as they were approaching Quiberon Bay near the Loire. Fortunately for the British, sustained violent winds from the northwest buffeted the French fleet, routinely disrupting its line, and providing boosts in speed and firing range. By the end of the day, the British had destroyed or captured seven ships including de Conflans's flagship, the *Soleil Royal*. French naval power was broken, the possibility of an invasion of England had been averted, and the Seven Years' War entered a new phase.

The vast distances covered by the American Revolution and the proximity of the Thirteen Colonies to the Atlantic Ocean ensured that wind would be a factor in the Continental victory as well. It is perhaps telling that the beginning of the Revolution was accompanied by a massive hurricane, the Independence Hurricane, which raged from Georgia to Virginia in 1775, causing much death and destruction and tearing the roof off of the Maryland State House. With the joining of the French to the American cause in 1778, Louis XVI dispatched a fleet under d'Estaing for operations in North American waters. London responded by launching its own squadron under Vice Admiral John Byron. Disease and a crew of inexperienced men slowed the British expedition, which was eventually overtaken by a massive storm in the Atlantic. The scattered and damaged ships limped into Sandy Hook in mid-August. The same storm system seems to have struck the fleets of d'Estaing and Howe as they prepared to do battle off of Rhode Island. Both forces were damaged and the French were unable to prevent British reinforcements from landing to stop Continental operations in Newport. Meanwhile, Byron's damage meant that he was unable to engage the weakened French fleet near Boston. He was subsequently hit by an additional storm and eventually forced to sail back to England.

Sir George Rodney had mixed luck when it came to the weather when his fleet sailed from England in 1780. The portion under his direct command, which turned south to battle the Spanish and lift the siege of Gibraltar, was aided by strong winds and the onset of night as it rounded the southern coast of Portugal. Two-thirds of the Spanish squadron was captured or sunk at the subsequent Battle of Cape St. Vincent, allowing for the British garrison to receive much-needed food and supplies. The second British squadron, which sailed for the West Indies, did not fare as well. The Great Hurricane of 1780, which tore through the southernmost Windward Islands and killed over twenty thousand people, struck the British navy with full force. The fury of the winds sank the *Stirling Castle, Phoenix, Andromeda, Deal Castle, Laurel, Scarborough, Barbados, Beaver Prize, Endeavor,* and *Victor.* The destruction of so many British ships would seriously alter the balance of power in the region and provide a boost for French efforts in the Caribbean.

The French Revolution and Napoleonic Wars continued to witness the impact of wind on various naval operations. Admiral Hugh Cloberry Christian had the task of sailing the as-yet largest British expedition to cross the Atlantic in 1795, aiming to engage the Dutch and French colonies around the Caribbean. Weather delayed the fleet until late in the fall, at which point a series of disastrous storms sank or damaged many of his ships as they made the journey. In the end it would take three attempts and six months before the expedition was able to make landfall at Barbados.

The French attempted to launch their own fleet in 1796, the purpose of which was to land some fifteen thousand men in Ireland and foment rebellion on the island against the British crown. General Louis Lazare Hoche and Admiral Morard de Galles duly organized an expedition of forty-four ships and planned to sail from Brest to Cork. The French knew that most of the British navy would return to port in winter to avoid the frequent storms of the Atlantic, thus allowing de Galles a chance of reaching Ireland. Auspiciously for the French invasion fleet, an approaching storm had caused the few present English ships to withdraw further away from the French coastline, presenting a limited window of opportunity for an unopposed descent upon Cork. Yet the British admiral had withdrawn for good reason: Not only was a storm bearing down on the Breton coast, but the winter of 1796 to 1797 proved to be one of the most violent in a century. By the time de Galles neared the Irish coast, twelve of his forty-four ships had sunk and the rest were scattered. The invasion proved to be a failure, and though the British navy was criticized for allowing the French free passage of the ocean, the wind had once again proven to be a valuable ally. Similar storms and unpredictable winds would help to keep the majority of Napoleon's invasion fleet bottled up in Boulogne for most of 1804 and 1805. Nor were the English spared from the horrors of storms at sea. The fame and bloodshed of Trafalgar was dwarfed by the loss of ships and lives during a violent storm immediately afterward. As Vice Admiral Collingwood reported to the Admiralty, "I can only say that in my life I never saw such efforts as were made to save these ships, and would rather fight another battle than pass through such a week as followed it."[116]

Nor were smaller bodies of water exempt from the effects of wind upon naval combat. During the War of 1812 the towns along the shores of Lake Erie were subject to constant invasion alarms, as British ships sailed on the water uncontested until Matthew Perry's victory in 1813. At one point early in the war, a raiding party of enemy craft approached the small settlement of Cleveland. As the panicked residents fled inland, a sudden calm overtook the lake and the squadron halted just short of the shoreline. The American militia used the next several hours to prepare defenses to counter any landing attempt. Suddenly a thunderstorm broke out in the afternoon, scattering the English ships and saving the town from attack. An American assault across the St. Lawrence around the same time was also turned away by violent winds, which blew for thirty-six hours. Finally, in September of 1813, Sir James Yeo allegedly used an approaching nor'easter to flee from an American squadron on Lake Ontario in what became termed the "Burlington Races."

Another battle during the War of 1812 affected by wind was the British assault on Sackett's Harbor. Serving as the headquarters of American naval forces on the Great Lakes, it was a tempting target for the British. Therefore, in May of 1813, when General George Prevost heard that the majority of American units in the region had moved against Ft. George, he seized the opportunity to attack Sackett's Harbor. Though the British held the advantage in number of ships and the quality of their troops, wind proved to be a powerful ally for the

Americans. Heavy winds kept the larger British ships out of cannon range of the shore, preventing them from reducing the American defenses. As one eyewitness recounted, "It was found impossible to take their forts without Artillery, which we had not with us—relying on the cooperation of the Navy which was prevented by an adverse wind."[117]

Yet the most important event of the war that hinged on the transitory nature of the wind was Perry's 1814 campaign on Lake Erie. The British fleet under Admiral Robert Barclay initially held the weather gauge, having sailed all night to gain a tactical advantage over the Americans. Yet, after emerging from Put-in Bay, the wind suddenly shifted. Perry's ships suddenly gained the upper hand and after hours of savage fighting and the loss of their command ship, the Americans were eventually victorious. The shift in the wind had given not only a great victory to the United States, but secured the entirety of the Great Lakes as well.

While the adoption of the steam engine mitigated some of the disastrous effects of wind on naval combat, it continued to play a role in land-based battles.[118] One of the more interesting episodes occurred shortly after the Battle of Bladensburg when a British army under Maj. Gen. Robert Ross occupied and burned the American capital at Washington, DC. Though President Madison was able to flee, the vast majority of the city was burned to the ground, along with the US government's buildings. Due to its recent construction, the firing of the town was more psychologically than strategically or economically damaging to the American cause. Suddenly, several hours after the fires were set by British sappers, a massive thunderstorm or hurricane touched down in Washington, putting out the great conflagration and disrupting English land and naval movements, resulting in more British deaths than had occurred during the occupation of the city. The "Storm that Saved Washington" may have become exaggerated in popular and national memory, but the concept of its providence did inspire generations to come, often a more important outcome.

Another popular account from the War of 1812, which collapses in the face of meteorological history, concerns the famous Star-Spangled Banner that flew over Fort McHenry. Francis Scott Key's ode to the flag that resisted the British bombardment upon the fort created not only the nation's official anthem, but a cult of worship around the banner itself. Yet the relic is not the actual pennant that flew over the fort throughout the night. As darkness fell, the commander of the fort, Major George Armistead, ordered the thirty-by-forty-foot flag lowered and replaced it with a much smaller storm flag. It was this standard which proudly waved over the bastion, defying the "rockets' red glare, the bombs bursting in air," throughout the night. As morning rose, Armistead re-raised the larger flag, the one which Key awoke to find still fluttering in the air, and which was eventually preserved in the Smithsonian Museum as the Star-Spangled Banner. The actual flag that defied the British has been lost to history.

Hurricanes continued to impact military operations in America during the Civil War. Much like the American Revolution, the first year of the conflict was visited, perhaps ominously, by a very active hurricane season. Rutherford B. Hayes, a major in the 23rd Ohio Regiment, wrote of the effects of one of the storms after the Battle of Carnifex Ferry to his wife. This particular hurricane was the fifth of the season, and had driven up the east coast of America in late September of 1861, impacting operations against the batteries at Fort Hatteras as well. Another storm in November would impact what was up to that point the largest amphibious operation in American history. The Navy Department, under much pressure from the government and the public, had hastily organized an expedition for the seizure of Port Royal in South Carolina. Though Captain Du Pont was concerned about the rushed nature of the operation, a timely storm that delayed his departure by a week allowed for further refinement of the mission. Yet once at sea, the American squadron was struck by a hurricane or tropical storm, scattering many of the ships and sinking or damaging several. It would take several days for the dispersed units to eventually coalesce

at Port Royal, and though the harbor was eventually taken, the expedition served to highlight the dangers the Navy would face in attempting
to apply the Anaconda Plan. This lesson would be further driven home
in December of 1862 when the famed USS *Monitor* sunk in a squall off
of the coast of the Carolinas and in May of 1863 when the USS *Amanda*
was scuttled by her crew after being damaged in a hurricane near the
Florida Panhandle.[119]

At Fort Fisher, a sudden winter storm at sea not only delayed a
Union attack, but also shielded the movement of hundreds of Confederate reinforcements from the mainland. By late 1864, Wilmington,
North Carolina was the last remaining Southern window to the world.
Its loss, along with Sherman's capture of the Deep South, would effectively isolate Lee in Virginia. Therefore, Lincoln approved a rather
audacious attempt to use a fire ship to breach the outer defenses of
the bastion and then land a subsequent amphibious assault. Though
General Grant and others doubted the efficacy of such a strategy, Benjamin Butler, the operation's commander, was more confident. Apart
from the questionable success of launching a bomb-laden ship at the
fort, the sudden onset of a fierce winter gale aided the Southerners
immensely. For three days the Union ships were kept at bay while
Confederate reinforcements were brought over from the mainland.
Braxton Bragg was able to almost triple the number of men under his
command behind the walls of Fort Fisher, and when combined with
the failure of the USS *Louisiana* to cause any damage to the walls of the
bastion when it exploded, proved to be more than a match for Butler's
assault.

A far more interesting wind-related phenomenon that proved to
be important during the conflict concerned acoustic propagation.
Landscape, wind, and weather can all have deleterious effects on the
transmission of sound, sometimes even producing disastrous results. In
February of 1862, Ulysses S. Grant almost ended his promising career at
its start due to his performance at the Battle of Fort Donelson. Early on
the morning of February 15, Grant proceeded downriver to meet with

Flag Officer Foote. In the meantime, the besieged Confederates under Pillow launched a breakout attempt aimed at the units under John A. McClernand. The combination of a fresh blanket of snow on the ground and adverse winds created an acoustic shadow over the battle-field, a rare phenomenon where sound waves are deflected or muffled, which kept Grant or Foote from hearing the gunfire that erupted. Only the unexpected withdrawal of Pillow back to the Southern trenches at Dover saved the situation, allowing Grant to return and launch a final assault on the fort. General Joseph E. Johnston would suffer a similar fate at the Battle of Seven Pines at the end of May, being unaware that McClellan had attacked his lines due to an acoustic shadow, despite being only two miles from the fighting. Further examples include the failure of Ord to aid Rosencrans's attack at Iuka in 1863, the muffling of Jackson's marching at Chancellorsville, and the failure of Ewell and Longstreet to coordinate against Round Top at Gettysburg. Overall, the issue of acoustics proved to be of fundamental importance in the waging of large-style campaigns in hilly country.[120]

Though naval ships by and large were able to counter many of the effects of wind with the advent of the modern steam engine, the expansion of warfare into new areas of technology once again made weather a factor in combat.[121] The American use of observational balloons during the Civil War often proved to be at the whim of gusts and strong storms, including the first balloon ever sent up by Thaddeus Lowe, the *Union*. Likewise, the reliance upon poison gas by both sides during World War I showed that once again weather was not an element that man could fully control.

Though officially outlawed by the Hague Conventions, the Germans eventually resorted to the use of lethal gas for a number of historical and strategic reasons. In April of 1915 the German army released a cloud of chlorine gas from six thousand prepositioned canisters at the start of the Battle of Ypres. The success of the tactic caught even them by surprise as they had not prepared to follow up effectively such a large breakthrough. Though many on both sides questioned the morality of employing the weapon, once it had been released all sides quickly began to use chemical arms. Wind unsurprisingly proved to be the largest uncontrollable factor in the release of gas by canisters. In this, the regular westerly winds that blew in the area hampered German gas operations. The German offensive at Ypres in 1915 relied heavily on meteorologists who coordinated with strategists in order to determine the best time to launch the operation. The obvious limitation on this was that entire campaigns could be delayed by days or weeks due to unfavorable winds, impacting other time-sensitive areas of the war as well. Both sides quickly moved toward shells to launch gas salvos in order to compensate for this, with the Germans completely phasing out canisters by 1916.

Clouds of gas could also drift into civilian areas, with thousands being killed over the course of the war. Worse yet, gas could just as easily blow back on the attacking army if the winds suddenly changed directions. Just this type of scenario unfolded in the fall of 1915 during the British assault on Loos. An initial gas attack by Field Marshal French proved to be not only ineffective, but blew back in the face of the advancing English soldiers, producing many casualties and leaving them unable to secure an initial breakthrough. A series of similar occurrences would unfold for the Germans at Rawka on the Eastern Front in June and July of 1915.

Although the belligerents attempted to study and more effectively utilize gas as a weapon, these efforts did not break the stalemate on the Western Front. An example of this scientific investigation into the use of gas can be found in an article written by B. C. Goss, a Lieutenant Colonel and Chief Gas Officer, for the Chemical Warfare Service in 1919. Goss suggested attacking in low winds where humidity was around 45 percent. "Temperature, wind, and humidity conditions, the hours between midnight and daylight are usually the most favorable for a gas attack, and, in addition, surprise is more easily possible at this time."[122]

During the interwar years, the desire for high-altitude precision bombing necessitated still better understanding of the effects of wind.

To help achieve this, the American and German governments invested heavily in developing a computerized bombsight in the 1920s and 1930s. The American version, the Norden Bombsight, was considered by many early in the war to be the key to Allied victory in Europe and the Pacific. Though in practice the results and accuracy of these machines were below what was promised, they represented an evolutionary step in the battle between man and the elements.

The air war over the Pacific was further affected by an additional weather factor, the Jet Stream. Japanese scientist Wasaburo Oishi first discovered the phenomenon in the 1920s, though his writings were largely unnoticed at the time. These strong winds, when combined with various weather fronts off of the Japanese islands, served to slow down American bombers heading westward across the Pacific, making them more inviting targets for defending Japanese aircraft. Tokyo took the Jet Stream into consideration early on, employing it to carry balloon bombs across the ocean toward America. Though these were by and large unsuccessful, they did serve as a useful psychological weapon. If the war had lasted longer, plans were under consideration to deliver chemical or biological components by this method as well.

Hurricanes and storms continued to wreak havoc during the Second World War as they had done in previous campaigns for centuries. Despite the window of pleasant weather that famously allowed for the landing at Normandy in 1944, a violent storm struck Omaha Beach on June 19, destroying one of the two Mulberry harbors that had been built by the Allies. These installations were meant to aid in the unloading of all supplies required to fuel the American and British push through France and the Low Countries. The sole remaining Mulberry, located at Arromanches, was reinforced and continued to handle the lion's share of material that arrived on the Continent for the next nine months.

Travel across the ocean during the war proved to be equally fraught with danger. In September of 1944 a massive category 3 storm raged up the Atlantic Seaboard, interfering with convoy shipping of war supplies to Europe. In what became known as the Great Atlantic Hurricane, five American naval ships sank, including the destroyer USS *Warrington*, and 344 men lost their lives. This situation was only magnified in the Pacific where a combination of more surface units, more amphibious operations, greater distances, and a lack of weather forecasting knowledge and ability invited disaster. As an example, in March of 1944, a typhoon downed the plane of the Japanese naval commander-in-chief, Mineichi Koga, as he flew near Palau.

In December of 1944, Typhoon Cobra bore down on the Third Fleet as Admiral Halsey sailed off the coast of the Philippines. Mistakenly heading into the heart of the storm, the fleet would end up suffering the loss of 3 destroyers, 146 planes, and 778 men. Almost six months later, Halsey again steered his ships into a storm, Typhoon Connie/Viper, this time having 33 ships damaged and losing 78 planes. The USS *Pittsburgh,* in particular, battled wind and waves for hours, losing her entire bow and 15 percent of her total length before limping back into harbor. Only because of the "wisdom and skill of the captain and the expert seamanship of her crew, not a single man had been lost or seriously injured."[123] Though the command ship USS *Ancon* was in the area and did radio warnings about the storm that it had picked up from both its own equipment and other meteorological sources, the process of decoding the messages meant that Halsey was not informed in time. A far greater storm, Typhoon Louise, bore down on Okinawa in October of 1945. Overall, 12 ships ran aground, 222 were driven ashore, and 36 men died, yet the greater damage was potential rather than actual. Had Japan not surrendered the month prior, the planned invasion of the islands was to begin in November of 1945. A storm in that region during the operation would have decimated the gathered resources and ships for the invasion armada. The US Navy would later report that, "If the war had not ended (when it did) this damage, especially the grounding and damage to 107 amphibious craft . . . would likely have seriously impacted the planned invasion of Japan."[124] The Divine Winds which had saved the islands from invasion in the thirteenth century and which the Japanese sought to technologically recreate with human torpedoes and kamikaze plans, could have actually materialized if the war had dragged on.

Even with the most modern of weather forecasting systems, storms continue to have both political as well as economic impacts, especially in underdeveloped countries. This is best exemplified by the 1970 Bhola Cyclone, which struck Bangladesh and killed an estimated five hundred thousand people. As it was part of Pakistan at the time, the citizens of the nation expected immediate help from Islamabad. When the military government in charge acted slowly in response, anger grew among the citizens of East Pakistan. In the ensuing months the opposition Awami League was elected to power precipitating the Bangladeshi Liberation War. The conflict soon spilled over into India as well, leading to the deaths of twelve thousand people and threatening to destabilize the Cold War in the region.

More recently in the Middle East, winds have come to play a role in American operations in both Iran and Iraq. An attempt to rescue American hostages in Tehran in 1979 was ultimately doomed in part by a haboob that helped to break up the rescue force's formation and delayed the arrival of units. During the Persian Gulf War in 1990, strong winds helped to prevent Saddam Hussein from utilizing his full contingent of Scud missiles and also dissuaded him in part from launching chemical or biological weapons against coalition forces. At the same time however, new studies suggest that coalition bombing sorties on Iraqi munition plants at Nasiriyah and Khamisiyah blew various chemical agents high enough into the atmosphere to carry them toward unsuspecting American troops in Saudi Arabia. Some researchers suggest that this may be the cause of the epidemic of Gulf War Syndrome that plagues veterans from the conflict.[125]

Overall, wind proved to be of particular interest in naval campaigns from ancient times until World War II. Historically, the side that gained the weather gauge had advantages in maneuverability and gunnery. This remained true even up to the Battle of the Denmark

Straits in 1941, where an outnumbered German naval unit was able to damage and elude a larger British fleet. Even with the advent of the steam engine, hurricanes and other storms at sea still proved powerful enough to wreak havoc on amphibious operations. Finally, campaigns waged on land in coastal areas could also be severely impacted, as seen in the case of the British attack on Washington in 1814. Thus, though wind may not have produced as many casualties as other types of weather phenomenon, its effect on movement, organization, and planning was vast.

6

SNOW AND HAIL

Have you entered the storehouses of the snow, or have you seen the storehouses of the hail, Which I have reserved for the time of distress, For the day of war and battle?
—JOB 38: 22–23

SNOW AND HAIL TENDED TO IMPACT war only in certain geographic regions. Likewise, as campaigns historically were only launched from spring until fall, snow had less of a chance to affect war than did rain or other elements. War tended to be avoided in winter for a number of reasons, one of which involved the destruction that could be wrought upon an army by cold and precipitation. Nor was this simply speculation on the part of classical commanders, as a number of historical battles were victim to just such conditions, enough to instill a healthy fear of campaigning in the dead of winter that would continue up until the twentieth century. In fact, even in the modern world, despite information on the impact of disease on the campaign notwithstanding, most blame winter and snow for the downfall of Napoleon in Russia.

Apart from the transportation or health issues associated with snow, hail bore a particularly destructive renown. The Bible emphasized the devastating effect of hail during a battle between Joshua and the Amorites. Following their defeat at the hands of the Israelites, the

Amorites fled from Bethoron to Azekah. The Bible recorded that, "As they fled before Israel on the road down from Beth Horon to Azekah, the LORD hurled large hailstones down on them, and more of them died from the hail than were killed by the swords of the Israelites."[126] The rarity of this type of event in the region and the amount of damage it caused were clearly the focus of the writer in an attempt to show divine favor for the Israelites.

Hail as a dangerous deterrent in war continued into the Middle Ages. In 1191, King Richard the Lionheart launched a determined assault on Jerusalem during the Third Crusade. Saladin had largely dispersed his forces, leaving the prized city exposed to siege. Weeks of heavy rainstorms and the onset of cold weather made the campaign untenable. Finally, at Beit Nuba, only a day's march from their destination, the Crusader army was caught in a hailstorm. The turn in weather, as well as the fear of being cut off from their supply lines should Saladin march to relieve the town, convinced Richard to call off the assault.

A similar event unfolded almost three centuries later as another English king launched a campaign against an enemy capital. Edward III had landed an army at Calais in 1359 and over the course of several months raided his way across northern France. As the French refused to give battle, the English monarch proceeded to ravage the outskirts of Paris in April of 1360. Suddenly, on what was to be remembered as Black Monday, as the English lay encamped outside of Chartres, a massive hailstorm pelted the army. Many men died in the ensuing chaos, with one chronicler recording that it was, "a foul day, full of myst and hayle, so that men dyed on horseback."[127] Edward apparently took the omen, coming as it did on Easter Monday, as a sign of God's displeasure at the violence of the war. He soon after resolved on signing a peace treaty with the French, the result of which, the Treaty of Bretigny, secured nine years of peace between the two countries.

For a number of reasons, hail is a far rarer event in weather than rain or snow. Therefore, its chances of impacting warfare are miniscule at best. More often the destruction of hail was confined to agriculture, which could devastate a nation or lead to wars in other ways. The outbreak of revolution in France was preceded by several severe hailstorms that destroyed crops and produced poverty and famine in the countryside and major cities. The French wine industry, a valuable contributor to the French economy, attempted numerous means by which to combat hail over the years, with perhaps the most risible being the development of hail cannons. As late as the start of the twentieth century, the French government was supplying powder to farmers in the belief that firing these canons would disrupt hail production.[128] Despite these limitations, as seen from the events at Jerusalem in 1191 and Paris in 1360, it is not completely absent from the annals of military history. The more common occurrence of snow, though not instantly as damaging as hail, produces more long-term problems for warfare.

One of the most celebrated stories of military daring and adventure is Xenophon's *Anabasis*. The classical work details the journey of a Greek mercenary army into the heart of the Persian Empire and its subsequent withdrawal toward the Black Sea in the year 401 BC. An entire chapter of the work recounts the time spent by the Greeks traversing the mountains of Armenia. Among the greatest hardships faced by the men throughout the entire expedition was the deep, freezing snow that delayed their progress. Xenophon recounted that, "The depth of the snow was a fathom, so that many of the baggage cattle and slaves perished, with about thirty of the soldiers."[129] Apart from immediate death, many subsequently succumbed to disease and frostbite: "From hence they marched through snow the whole of the following day, and many of the men contracted the *bulimia* . . . Such of the soldiers, also, as had lost their sight from the effects of the snow, or had had their toes mortified by the cold, were left behind."[130] Two thousand years later questions still remain as to why the Greeks would purposefully march into such a region, knowing full well the damage that could be caused by snow and ice, with many even doubting the veracity of Xenophon's work.[131] The Romans would also suffer in the same region centuries later. The general Lucullus lost control of his men while campaigning in the Armenian winter in 67 BC, a situation that helped to start the rise to prominence of Pompey the Great. Finally, in the early third century, Severus Alexander suffered a series of weather-related setbacks while fighting the Persians there as well. Armenia and the Caucasus Mountains became both a symbolic and political edge to the civilized world. Perhaps not surprisingly it was also the location where the ancients chose to place Prometheus in chains for his eternal punishment.

In the same vein as rain, snow tended to have the greatest impact on war in terms of the movement of troops. Nowhere was this more exemplified in the classical world than in the march of Hannibal across the Alps. While the transportation of tens of thousands of men across these treacherous mountains at any time of year would have been celebrated, Hannibal's completion of it in the late fall and early winter was even more remarkable. Not only did the snow and ice hamper movement, according to Polybius the various Spanish and African troops were actually terrified at the sight of the conditions around them, with many deserting. Snow drifts and treacherous conditions cost him as many men in the descent of the mountains as during the initial ascent in which they were under attack from local tribes.[132] In all, Hannibal lost the vast majority of his army to the snows and ice of the Alps, including many of his feared elephants. Despite this, the Carthaginian commander was able to decisively defeat the Romans at two winter battles, near the Ticinus and Trebia rivers. Yet, snow was once again on the side of Rome, helping to kill off all but one of his elephants following Hannibal's victory at the Trebia River.[133]

Hannibal was not the only leader who would see his force and campaign impacted by the treacherous snow of the Alps. Centuries later, a declining Rome witnessed its emperor, Majorian, struggling to move his largely non-Roman army across the snows of the Alps, "sounding with his long staff the depth of the ice or snow."[134] Much like Hannibal, Majorian was able to move enough men over the mountains to launch his subsequent campaign, recovering much of Gaul and Hispania from the recent German invasions in the process. The Russian general Alexander Suvorov and French general Jacques Macdonald also famously led marches over the snowcapped peaks, losing many men in the process. Learning from these previous lessons, Napoleon organized a much more successful crossing of the mountain range in 1800. Sending his men over in small groups, providing ample food and drink, and choosing the month of May to make the transit, his crossing caught the Austrians by surprise and helped to secure the peninsula for France.

The Battle of Towton emerges yet again as an engagement thoroughly molded by the elements. Several days of light snow rendered the cannon brought out from London ineffective, and also weakened the bowstrings of the archers, much as the rains of the Teutoburg Forest did to the Romans. Once battle was joined, the increasingly heavy snow flew directly into the eyes of the Lancastrian troops. Therefore, not only were Somerset's archers unable to aim properly, when combined with the strong winds on the battlefield, their arrows fell harmlessly in front of the Yorkist lines. Still later, the snow turned the Lancastrian retreat into a massacre as the swollen Cock Beck stream became a raging river. Many drowned attempting to escape the battlefield, which was the bloodiest in English history.

The Great Northern War, which raged from 1700 to 1721, was fought in a region in which cold temperatures and snowy weather was bound to impact combat. Peter the Great quickly moved against the Swedish city of Narva in modern day Estonia, besieging it late in the fall. As the other enemy armies had largely gone into winter camps, Charles XII decided to engage the Russian army first. Outnumbered almost four to one by an entrenched opponent, the Swedish took an enormous gamble by launching a direct assault on the Russian lines. The insanity of the plan, when combined with the onset of a blizzard, moved many of the Swedish commanders to push for postponing the battle. Charles XII is said to have exclaimed, "No! The snow is at our backs, but full in the enemy's faces."[135] Charles XII advanced his men silently until they overwhelmed the Russian lines, sending the Slavic army into disarray. The snow blew hard into the faces and eyes of the Russians, blinding them and causing them to shoot wildly above the advancing Swedes. Charles XII killed or captured nearly thirty thousand of the thirty-seven-thousand-man Russian army, saving Narva and propelling Charles to international renown for his martial skills.

The Siege of Fredriksten in 1718, though usually known for the death of King Charles XII and the subsequent dénouement of the Great Northern War, witnessed far more loss due to snow than simply the death of the monarch. The decision by the Swedish ruler to besiege the city in the autumn of that year proved to be disastrous, as the quickly freezing ground made the digging of trenches nearly impossible. Following the death of their king and the lifting of the siege, Carl Gustaf Armfeldt led a portion of the army back to Sweden on what became known as the Carolean Death March. A series of snowstorms and a blizzard struck the withdrawing army as it crossed the hills of Norway. By the time the surviving soldiers made it home, nearly two-thirds of the six-thousand-man army were dead, mostly from hypothermia, while another six hundred were crippled for life with severe frostbite. Sweden's century of expansion had come to an end.

The Battle of Mollwitz in 1741, at which Frederick the Great received his baptism by fire, almost proved to be his last battle as well, due to a number of tactical errors made worse by the presence of heavy snow. As Thomas Carlyle later described the conditions on the battlefield, "it still snows and blows; you cannot see a yard before you."[136] While fog and snow allowed the Prussians to advance unnoticed by the Austrians, the fresh blanket of powder on the ground caused Frederick to incorrectly position his men. Only an equal number of mistakes by the Austrians, when combined with the training of the Prussian infantry and the leadership of Count Schwerin, allowed Frederick to snatch victory from the snowy jaws of defeat.

As described previously, campaigning in winter was often more an act of desperation than of sound planning. It was just such a concern that pushed General Richard Montgomery to coordinate his attack on the walls of Quebec with an impending snowstorm. The American seizure of Montreal had come very late in the year, but a determined Montgomery decided to assault Quebec before the year was out. On December 31, 1775, American units attempted to use a heavy snowstorm to mask their two-pronged approach to the city. This was necessitated in part to the paucity of numbers on the American side. In the end, the assaults led by Montgomery and Arnold were more hindered than helped by the snow. The former commander was killed, the latter commander was wounded, and the city of Quebec remained firmly under British control. America's hopes of joining Canada to the rebellion failed.

American and British units would encounter similar hardships a generation later during the War of 1812. The early onset of winter along the Canadian border meant that campaign seasons had to be adjusted accordingly or else affected by the harsh cold and unrelenting snow that would accumulate in the region. As of 1801, the British army had adopted the wearing of "great coats" by its soldiers in winter climates in order to reduce the impact of disease and desertion. The lack of such winter equipment by the Americans, who relied on personally funded gear, certainly lent a tactical advantage to the United Kingdom.

The advent of the Napoleonic Wars inaugurated many new martial ideas and tactics. In addition, it saw a number of campaigns that were unorthodox in timing or manner. A number of these included engagements that were fought in winter, often plagued by blinding snowstorms. In December of 1800 at the Battle of Hohenlinden, the French general Moreau was able to defeat a larger Austrian opponent in part due to the effects of the snow upon the enemy's ability to coordinate the arrival of units on the battlefield. English poet Thomas Campbell immortalized the scene as . . .

And redder yet those fires shall glow
On Linden's hills of blood-stained snow,

And darker yet shall be the flow

Of Iser, rolling rapidly.[137]

Napoleon himself would campaign extensively in winter months especially during the War of the Fourth Coalition as he sought to push eastward and destroy the Prussian units left remaining after Jena-Auerstedt. In February of 1807 his army collided with a Russian force under Count von Bennigsen at the Battle of Eylau in East Prussia. Heavy snow prevented Marshal Ney from hearing of the battle until well into the day, delaying his arrival on the field. By the end of the engagement both sides had little to show for fifty thousand casualties lying in the snow. Weather proved to be one of the few things that could slow down the French juggernaut.

Napoleon's issues with snow continued as he moved east, culminating in the disaster that was to befall his army during the campaign in Russia in 1812. In this he was largely repeating the mistake of Charles XII of Sweden who marched into the country over a hundred years prior in 1709. Blizzard conditions and snow caused the deaths of thousands of Swedes and soon led to the declaration of a cease-fire by both sides until the end of winter. Over a century after Napoleon retreated from Moscow, Hitler was forced to follow a similar path as snow likewise crippled his own invasion, obstructing the movement of tanks and supplies and causing an enormous number of cases of frostbite. Perhaps ironically, a series of disastrous hailstorms had helped to sufficiently damage the harvests of the French peasants enough to push them into rebellion in the first place back during the 1780s.

Even a people long associated with snowy weather could see their best-laid plans thrown into ruin by its approach. Ever since the British secured the subcontinent of India, various European nations including the French, the Germans, and even the Russians sought to seize it as a means of weakening their rival. Perhaps none were better situated for just such a campaign than the Russians in 1801. Czar Paul I collaborated with Napoleon to launch a joint offensive against the lightly defended crown jewel of the British Empire. An advance force of Don Cossacks under their leader, Vasily Petrovich Orlov, left the town of Orenburg and proceeded toward Khiva. Yet, a harsh winter the year before reduced forage for the horses while heavy snows slowed down their movement. Warming weather did little to improve the condition of the march, flooding fields and overflowing rivers and streams.[138] These unfavorable conditions and the concurrent assassination of Paul I led to the abandonment of the invasion after only seven hundred kilometers. The Russians had perhaps come closer to any other modern nation in their efforts to expel the British from India, but unrealistic goals, poor planning, and harsh weather proved to be their undoing.

By and large, nations continued to shun large-scale campaigning in winter throughout the nineteenth century, yet with the advent of total war during the twentieth century, this often became unavoidable. The First World War, with its continuous trench warfare on the Western Front, saw men beset by the weather challenges of all four seasons. Movement in the cold of winter or following a particularly heavy snowstorm was difficult as the men would be unable to dig new trench lines to consolidate their gains. Yet, in the first winter of the conflict numerous offensives, including the First Battle of Artois, the First Battle of Champagne, the Battle of Hartmannswillerkopf, and the Second Battle of the Masurian Lakes all occurred in the dead of winter. The last of these, that at the Masurian Lakes, saw German soldiers advancing through five-foot-tall snow drifts in an attempt to push the Russians back over the Vistula River.

While the Eastern Front experienced more fluid battles, the unforgiving terrain of the Carpathian Mountains separating Russia from Austria-Hungary meant that winter warfare was to be a major factor in the first year of the war. An Austrian attempt to drive the Russians from the mountains in January and February of 1915 produced little but frozen casualties. As one officer recounted, "Fog and heavy snow falls, we have lost all sense of direction; entire regiments are getting lost, resulting in catastrophic losses."[139] As the war progressed however, the launching of winter offensives lessened. As demonstrated by the difficulties faced during the early offensives of 1914–1915 and by the Germans at Verdun in 1916, frozen ground and snow combined to lessen the effectiveness of operations.

The Second World War experienced similar winter combat to the First, especially in Arctic areas. Initial Japanese attempts to seize the Aleutian Islands and to raid Dutch Harbor were consistently impacted by fog, snow, and ice flows. Likewise, American and Canadian operations to expel the Japanese would suffer more casualties from frostbite and other weather-related deaths and injuries than from bullets. In addition, the deep snows of the region made the use of vehicles nearly impossible, resulting in small-unit infantry engagements and one of the last banzai attacks of the war. Likewise, though Hitler hoped that his offensive into the Ardennes in late 1944 to early 1945 would be aided by the fog and snow that normally blanketed the area, by December 22, heavy snow and freezing temperatures were actually negatively impacting both sides. Significant snowfall ruined road networks and kept the Germans from transporting men and matériel to the front. Freezing soldiers tore up snow fences to use as firewood, further hampering Nazi efforts to clear the roads for reinforcements. Close to twenty thousand Allied soldiers alone would be hospitalized for cold-related injuries during the battle—as many as would be wounded by bullets.

The Cold War, true to its name, saw a number of engagements fought in traditionally inhospitable regions that had normally been avoided by other generals and leaders. Korea remains the most obvious example, with cold, frostbite, and snow impacting much of the combat between the two sides. Less well-known are the wars between India, Pakistan, and China that took place astride the Himalaya Mountains. The Sino-Indian War of 1962 involved a lightning-quick advance by Beijing in an effort to expel Indian units from disputed territory. Though Chinese historiography portrays the one-month conflict as ending due to the achievement of its goals, the more poignant reason for its termination rests with the snow of the Himalayan winter. In fact, the very celerity with which China undertook its attack was due in large part to concerns over the effect that the heavy snows of the area would have upon its ability to move men and supplies. Learning from its mistakes, India timed the launching of its own war with Pakistan in 1971 to coincide with the closing of the Himalayan passes to snow in order to prevent China from aiding the latter country.

Snow, much like rain, affected war in terms of both movement and casualties. From the march of Hannibal's men over the Alps, to the Chinese in Tibet, the transportation of men and matériel over snow-covered territory has always been a near-impossible encumbrance in war. Likewise, attempts to do so have very often produced mass casualties from frostbite or related conditions. The various failed invasions of Russia, the tragedies suffered at numerous winter encampments, and more specifically the disastrous British withdrawal from Kabul in 1842 during which the cold and snow killed thousands, all bear witness to the power of snow.

Yet, the general lack of available food for foraging during the winter restricted the actual number of campaigns launched for thousands of years. Only recently with the advent of air power, the production of winter gear, the ability to enforce supply lines, and the prevalence of permanent war has campaigning in the snow become more common.

7

HEAT

Heat not a furnace for your foe so hot
That it do singe yourself.
—WILLIAM SHAKESPEARE, *HENRY VIII*

THOUGH RAIN AND SNOW MAY HAMPER campaigns or potentially lead
to casualty-inducing diseases, few weather phenomena are as immediately damaging as heat. The enervating effect of heat on soldiers, both
in combat and on campaign, is well documented. High temperatures
quickly produce massive casualties through heatstroke, incapacitating
armies and compromising offensives. Some of this is clearly geographically dependent, arising as an issue in warmer regions. Often the effect
of heat was particularly troublesome to foreign foes unaccustomed to
the warmer climes in which they found themselves engaged. Just as
frequently though, the heavy uniforms, armor, and equipment of local
armies could also leave them open to the debilitating effects of their
own local climate.

The Book of Joshua contains an account of a battle between the Israelites and the Amorites that has long plagued Biblical literalists. Chapter
10, verse 13 describes an engagement between the two armies at Gibeon:

> So the sun stood still, and the moon stopped, till the nation avenged
> itself on its enemies, as it is written in the Book of Jashar. The sun

stopped in the middle of the sky and delayed going down about a full day.

While men such as Galileo and Calvin have attempted to prove or refute the notion that either the movement of the sun or earth stopped to allow for the Hebrews to slaughter more of their enemy, the poetry suggests a more practical issue. The Amorites were a well-organized polity at the time with well-regarded armies and armor. Their soldiers at the Battle of Gibeon would have armor with metal shields, helmets, and breastplates, while the more technologically primitive Israelites would have worn everyday clothing or used leather armor. The notion of a stalled sun may have instead referred to the debilitating effects of the sun upon the heavily armored Amorites. The successful march of the Hebrews from Egypt through the land of Canaan may have actually owed more to their use of lighter armor than to divine favor.

Perhaps the greatest empire to inhabit the region of the Middle East, the Persian Empire, routinely had to deal with the issue of high temperatures in battle. The son of Cyrus the Great, Cambyses II, expanded his father's empire in multiple directions. Yet his army was famously defeated by the heat and sand of the Libyan desert. According to Herodotus, the Great King dispatched an army of tens of thousands of men toward the Siwa Oasis. As they trekked across the vast desert however, sandstorms and raging temperatures allegedly destroyed the entire expedition, despite their penchant for lighter armor and wicker shields. Ironically, a century later this lighter equipment designed for the temperature conditions of the Middle East left the Persians at a distinct disadvantage during their wars in Greece. The heavier metal armor and shields of the Athenians and Spartans compensated for the smaller size of their armies in various engagements against the Persians.

The tables would be turned upon the Greeks a century later during their own invasion of the Persian Empire. Alexander's initial forays into the Near East took place during the cooler months of the year and he avoided offensive campaigns in Egypt altogether after the Siege of Gaza, when the entire region rose in revolt against the Persians. Heat directed his march toward a final battle with Darius as well, with Alexander choosing a more northerly route after crossing the Euphrates, rather than moving directly against Babylon. When the young Macedonian king finally did meet his rival in battle at Gaugamela, he did so in early October, though this was more likely due to luck and accident than careful planning. Yet, Alexander's meteorological luck and his men's tolerance to heat finally failed as the Macedonians campaigned in Bactria. Quintus Curtius Rufus wrote that "the heat of the summer sun scorches the sands and, when these start to heat up, everything on them is baked as if by perpetual fire . . . So it was their resolution that failed first, and then their bodies."[140] Alexander the Great's army, defeated by no foe, was brought to its knees by heat. The great conqueror himself would finally die six years later in Babylon attempting to consolidate his new empire. While theories surrounding his death have been dominated by allegations of poisoning, others have contended that heatstroke or malaria picked up during his time in warmer climes were the more probable culprits.

Malaria and hot conditions often went hand in hand, crippling many armies and ruining numerous campaigns. One of the most notable involved the defeat of Antony and Cleopatra at Actium in 31 BC. Occupying Greece since the year before, Antony and his men settled down into winter camps to await reinforcements and an opening for action. Unfortunately, the onset of exceedingly hot and muggy summer weather brought malaria into the camp, decimating his ranks. Far from simply reducing the number of men he was able to commit to battle, these losses impacted him tactically by depriving him of the use of his largest ships. The majority of his fleet was composed of octaries, or eight-bank rowing vessels, which relied on ramming as their primary means of combat. The subsequent reduction in the number of rowers available to him meant that these large ships were more of a hindrance than a benefit. By the end of the day the vast majority of his ships were sunk or burning and thousands of Romans and Greeks lay in the water. Antony and Cleopatra quickly retreated to Egypt, defeated more by heat and malaria than by the legions of Octavius. Heat-related illness would also be the bane of British, Spanish, and American troops in Cuba and around the Caribbean as well in the eighteenth and nineteenth centuries.

The Romans faced many of the same temperature-related hardships as the Greeks as they sought to expand across the Middle East. In 24 BC a Roman expeditionary force under the prefect of Egypt, Gaius Aelius Gallus, marched from Alexandria toward the area of modern-day Yemen. Known as Arabia Felix at the time, the region was the center of the incense trade and would have proven quite valuable if it could be conquered. Roman historians claimed that Gallus was misled by local guides and became lost in the sands of western Arabia. "The larger part of the army perished," Dio Cassius records, due to heatstroke for which the only remedy available was the consumption of wine.[141] In the end, the entire expedition was ultimately a failure and established the natural extent of the Roman Empire in that region.[142]

The hot temperatures of the region likewise confronted Emperor Trajan's last major war of conquest during his invasion of Parthia in 113 AD. Despite some initial progress, by 116 the war had dragged to a halt before the fortress of Hatra on the Tigis River. Months of siege failed to take the city and the ever-increasing temperatures seem to have taken their toll on Trajan. His health was beginning to suffer, possibly as a result of heatstroke or disease. The outbreak of a Jewish revolt further west provided a convenient excuse for the withdrawal of his armies back to the Mediterranean. By 117, Trajan was dead and so were the hopes of Roman expansion beyond Mesopotamia or the seizure of the Persian Gulf.

Nor was the Middle East the sole region where heat played a factor in battle. Often even slightly warmer weather enervated a more northerly foe when facing a southern opponent. Such was the case, according to Plutarch, of the Cimbri as they faced Marius at the Battle of Vercellae:

> The Romans were favoured in the struggle, Sulla says, by the heat, and by the sun, which shone in the faces of the Cimbri. For the Barbarians were well able to endure cold, and had been brought up in shady and chilly regions, as I have said. They were therefore undone by the heat; they sweated profusely, breathed with difficulty, and were forced to hold their shields before their faces. For the battle was fought after the summer solstice . . . And their bodies were so inured to toil and so thoroughly trained that not a Roman was observed to sweat or pant, in spite of the great heat and the run with which they came to the encounter.[143]

For the Norwegian army under Harald Hardrada, which landed in northeastern England in 1066, the late-summer warmth was just as oppressive as the Romans found Arabia or the Cimbri northern Italy. After making landfall, the Vikings assumed that King Harold of England was much further south and were completely unprepared for battle. In fact, most of Harald's soldiers had removed their armor in a bid to avoid the oppressive heat of the day, with many soldiers apparently succumbing to heatstroke. Thus the sudden appearance of the Anglo-Saxons caught the Norwegians by surprise. Outnumbered and largely unarmored, the Vikings were slaughtered by the English at Stamford Bridge. Though the battle is often overshadowed by the subsequent loss of England to the Normans at Hastings a few weeks later, the quick thinking of Harold and the heat of a late English summer had largely ended the Viking threat to the British Isles that had dominated the region for centuries.

The return of European warriors to the Middle East with the onset of the Crusades provided ample opportunities for heat-related illnesses and battles to be affected by temperature. Contrary to much popular opinion it was not the metal composition of the knights' armor that caused heat-related problems, but rather its weight. Chainmail, which had been employed since Roman times, ventilated heat from the body and helped to keep its wearer cool by acting as a heat sink. Learning early on from experience, the Crusaders would also often soak their gambeson or cloth padding in water to help further cool their bodies before battle. Therefore, access to a source of water was vital on any campaign, and in the arid conditions of the Near East could prove to be the deciding factor in any attempt to secure both Jerusalem and the larger region. Such a scenario unfolded in 1187 when King Guy of Jerusalem and his army confronted Saladin at the Horns of Hattin. The Sultan of Egypt schemed to lure the Christian army away from its camp at the Sephoria fountain by besieging the nearby city of Tiberias. Guy and Raymond III of Tripoli foolishly plunged into the arid region between the two forces, approaching Hattin where Saladin held them off for days while they slowly succumbed to heat exhaustion and dehydration in their heavy armor. As recorded in *The Old French Continuation of William of Tyre*:

> The heat was so great that they could not go on so as to reach water.
> . . . As soon as they had made camp, Saladin ordered his men to collect brushwood, dry grass, stubble and anything else that could be used to light fires, and to make palisades all round the Christian host. This command was carried out in full. Early next morning he ordered the fires to be lit. This was quickly done. The fires burned vigorously and made an enormous amount of smoke, and this, in addition to the heat of the sun, caused the Christians considerable discomfort and harm. Saladin had commanded caravans of camels loaded with water from the Sea of Tiberias to be brought up and had the water jars positioned near the camp. They were then emptied in the sight of the Christians with the result that they and their horses suffered even greater anguish through thirst.[144]

The work goes on to recount that the horses of the Crusaders also suffered, which would not only have crippled the cavalry of the army but also prevented their ability to effectively escape and evade the Muslim army.[145] After much slaughter, the European army was defeated and Saladin remained master of the Near East. It is perhaps telling that upon capturing King Guy, the Egyptian ruler offered him his own cup of chilled water to relieve his overbearing thirst. "The king was very hot and thirsty, and the sultan gave him snow-covered water to drink."[146]

A similar situation unfolded over six centuries later in the same region during the Glorious Revolution. After securing much of England, William of Orange had dispatched Marshal Frederick Schomberg to Ireland in order to subdue the island and rout the remaining armies of James II. The general was confronted by unforgiving weather and his troops suffered heavily from disease. Frustrated at Schomberg's inaction, William himself landed in 1690 and defeated James at the Battle of the Boyne. Despite later aggrandizement of the engagement, unseasonably warm weather on July 1 caused heat exhaustion among his men and horses and allowed the Catholic forces of James to successfully withdraw with only minor losses. In fact, the war would drag on for another year, involving several more battles and bloody sieges that belied the nickname of the Bloodless Revolution.[147]

While the vast majority of the success of the Spanish in conquering much of the New World is due to the unintended impact of disease upon the natives of the region, temperature played an underappreciated role as well. Due to a combination of a lack of technological skill and the high temperatures and humidity of the region, the various Mesoamerican civilizations and tribes tended to employ light cotton or wood- or plant-based armor. Though the Spanish certainly were hindered in the heat of Mexico and Central America due to their metal armor, their steel swords and shields, designed around the idea of the heavier armor used in cooler European temperatures, proved to be more than a match for the cotton armor of the Aztec.[148] In fact, the history of the Spanish and various other European groups fighting in a variety of landscapes made them more adaptable to battlefield temperatures than some of the more sedentary tribes and kingdoms that they came across during the Age of Exploration.

As with most other forms of weather-related interference, technology often proved vital in countering the negative effects of heat. As far back as 1503, a Spanish army under Gonzalo de Cordoba was able to defeat an opposing French force despite suffering immensely from heatstroke and dehydration. Weeks of marching in warm weather along with a lack of water had reduced the Spanish army to dire straits. Despite both its physical condition and smaller size—the Spanish force was vastly outnumbered by the French under the Duke of Nemours—de Cordoba achieved a tremendous and lopsided victory at the Battle of Cerignola by using defensive measures to slow down the advance of the French and deploying an overwhelming number of musket-carrying infantry.

One of the most famous heat-related battles in American history was fought at Monmouth in late June of 1778. A five-day heat wave blanketed New Jersey with temperatures peaking at 100 degrees on the day of the engagement. The woolen coats and packs of the British and German soldiers would have only added to their misery, with apocryphal tales rising of men rushing to drink out of stagnant pools of water on the battlefield. Unlike their Scottish cousins at the Battle of Mechelen in 1578, the British would not simply undress and fight in more comfortable fashion. Washington himself chose to march his men at night to both achieve the element of surprise and to avoid the worst of the heat, unfortunately these efforts also served to disperse his army and almost proved to be disastrous during the early part of the fight. By the time the longest battle of the Revolution was over, English General Clinton recorded fifty-nine deaths from heatstroke, a number almost equal to losses from bullets. A final legend associated with the battle is the tale of Molly Pitcher. Believed to actually be Mary Ludwig Hays, she and other women carried water to the battlefield to help cool the men and the overheated cannon. The high temperatures of the day not only helped to shape this important battle, but also created an iconic figure who would become a mainstay of the early feminist movement. Likewise, their efforts showed the advantage that could be gained with respect to weather conditions by local forces employing local provisions.

A generation later, heatstroke was once again a cause of concern in a war between America and the United Kingdom. Following its seizure of the Chesapeake Bay in August of 1814, the British navy landed a 4,500-man force under Major General Robert Ross for a march on Washington, DC. The ensuing Battle of Bladensburg has been termed by many as the "greatest disgrace ever dealt to American arms." In fact, the stiffest resistance to Ross's men came not from the muskets of the various ill-trained militia groups, but the 98 degree weather that day in Maryland. The vast majority of the nearly 250 casualties on the British side were from heatstroke, with many more cases perhaps going unreported. The excessive temperatures and forced marches reduced the ability, discipline, and morale of the British soldiers. Fears that the excessive heat would usher in an outbreak of Yellow Fever prompted Admiral Cochrane to order an early withdrawal from the Bay.[149] Washington and its treasures were saved more by hurricanes, heat, and fears of disease than by the efforts of President Madison and his wife.

The Age of Imperialism brought with it further wars and battles in lands that often experienced extremes of heat. Napoleon's men suffered extraordinarily in the heat of the Egyptian dessert in 1798 as they fought their way toward Cairo under the summer sun. The British would experience similar conditions in India as they attempted to pacify that region. British confronted the debilitating effect of tropical heat during several notable expeditions, including those of Sir Charles James Napier in 1843 and Lord Dalhousie in 1848, as well as a war in Burma in 1853. In the 1848 Second Anglo-Sikh War, 175 men of the 32nd Cornwall Regiment fell ill during that unit's time in Punjab while 14 died of heatstroke.[150] Britain's imperial success came in part from their ability to learn from their experiences. This is demonstrated by the Earl Roberts's effective use of early-morning marching to avoid temperatures that reached over 100 degrees as he moved to relieve Kandahar in 1880. Many of these lessons would be repeated a generation later during the Boer War. By the end of the century, the British had adopted lighter uniforms, khaki summer outfits, larger canteens, and more easily carried personal equipment.

In a repetition of history, the heavy clothing and uniforms of Western armies served as an added disadvantage when waging war in tropical climates. This was even the case during the American Civil War where the wool uniforms favored by the Union were less suited to the warmer summers of the South than the cotton uniforms of the Confederates. This was particularly true at Gettysburg where temperatures in the high 70s and 80s led to a number of cases of heatstroke. Nearly forty years later, American soldiers in the Philippines took to abandoning their khaki jackets in favor of the more conspicuous, but cooler, blue campaign shirt. During this war the casualties from heatstroke sometimes topped those from actual battles. Over 3 percent of the men in Colorado's Volunteer Infantry Regiment succumbed to heatstroke. The true extent of casualties from heat were most likely much higher, as the units kept poor records related to heatstroke victims.[151]

The same held true even in more undeveloped areas. Shaka's first major victory as part of his Mfecane owed as much to heat as it did to his strategy. The Zulu army was positioned on Gqokli Hill in May of 1818 as a much more numerous Ndwandwe force advanced against them. Yet the enemy had marched all day in the hot sun and had consumed the vast majority of its water supply. Shaka, on the other hand, had stockpiled food and water on the hill and kept his well-rested men hydrated. After numerous charges, many Ndwandwe soldiers began to desert in order to find fresh drinking water. The Zulu were able to survive the assaults and carried the day. Shaka's march to tribal domination had begun.

At the same time poor choices of equipment could increase the likelihood of succumbing to heatstroke. Out of all of the cases of heatstroke experienced by the German army on the Western Front in the First World War, 40 percent occurred during the first month of the conflict.[152] While some of this was due to the rapid advances of the Prussian soldiers during August, at a pace never repeated for the remainder of the conflict, part of it also arose from their choice of headgear. The heavy leather German *Pickelhaube*, would have retained the sun's heat and had little ventilation, leaving the German soldiers sweaty and more susceptible to heatstroke.

The global nature of the World Wars saw Western armies again exposed to the harsh heat of the Middle East and other areas. General Frederick Maude was faced with temperatures in excess of 120 degrees when his British army attempted to attack the town of Ramadi, Iraq during the Mesopotamian Campaign of 1917. Heatstroke was such a real concern that the British relied on motorized transportation to move the men across the desert at night. The first assault in July proved to be a failure, with 321 of the 566 English casualties resulting directly from the heat. It would take a significant number of reinforcements and over two months before Ramadi was finally in Allied hands. Even medical men were victims of the deadly effect of heat in the region. Dr. Victor Horsley, the famed neurosurgeon, died of heatstroke while in Iraq in July of 1916. Fatalities from heat occurred in World War II as well, yet due to a better understanding of the causes and treatment of the condition, total casualties throughout the war for the Allies were under 250.[153]

Nor did the cooling waters of the sea provide relief. In fact, the exposed conditions common to naval warfare have led to numerous deaths from heat over the past several centuries. Even at the relatively bloodless Battle of Manila Bay in 1898, the sole American casualty arose from heatstroke rather than the gunnery of the Spanish. Rivers could prove deadly as well, as in August of 1866 when the crew of the USS *Wachusett* suffered immensely from heat exhaustion while sailing up the Yangtze River. The commander of the vessel, Captain Robert Townsend, died from heatstroke and the boat was forced to retreat downriver to the safety of Shanghai.

Despite many advances in both technology and medicine, the increasing frequency of wars in tropical and desert climates has allowed heatstroke to remain a factor of concern in combat. During the Six-Day War many Egyptian soldiers perished from heatstroke and dehydration as they attempted to flee across the open desert from the rapidly approaching Israeli army. Heatstroke presented a problem for American soldiers in Vietnam as well. At the Battle of No Goi Island, for example, twice as many Marines were evacuated with heatstroke than with injuries from battle. Finally, coalition forces fighting to liberate Kuwait in 1991 were forced to wear heavy chemical warfare suits due to fear that Saddam Hussein would employ these banned weapons against them. Though protected against casualties from these weapons, temperatures inside the MOPP suit could reach well over 120 degrees in the Iraqi desert.

Though heat tended to be a geographically contained weather phenomenon in warfare, at certain times it could strike armies elsewhere as well, as illustrated by the Battle of Monmouth and the Battle of Stamford Bridge. The prevalence of conflicts in Africa, Latin America, the Middle East, and Southeast Asia after World War II have meant that heatstroke and other issues related to high temperatures will continue to be active components of warfare for the foreseeable future.

8

COLD

A clear, cold Christmas, lovely weather for killing
Germans.
—GEORGE S. PATTON, 1944

WHILE SNOW AND COLD TEMPERATURES NORMALLY went hand-in-hand
as weather issues confronting armies in history, the latter was more
likely to occur on its own. Much as with heat, cold introduces elements of physical discomfort, health concern, the obstruction of movement, disease, and death. In fact, the cold of winter had dictated the
campaign seasons of combat in Europe and numerous other locations
around the world for thousands of years. Even in the modern era, frost
and low temperatures can wreak havoc with the most advanced of
equipment.

One of the earliest accounts of winter directing the timeline of a
campaign arises during the Peloponnesian War. Athens launched a
controversial expedition in 415 BC to attack the island of Sicily. Landing at the start of winter, the Athenian soldiers launched a swift assault
on Syracuse, but after failure to secure the town, they withdrew to
camps around Catana. The break in action caused by the descent of
winter allowed the Syracusians to acquire reinforcements and support
from various city-states, most notably Sparta. This delay proved to be

costly to the Athenians, and when combined with a number of other factors ultimately served to doom their expedition.

While Hannibal and the Carthaginians suffered similar afflictions from cold while campaigning in the Alps and northern Italy, it was actually the Roman inhabitants of the region who would bear the brunt of their own climate. On the day of the winter solstice in 218 BC, a Roman army under the command of Tiberius Sempronius Longus faced Hannibal across the partially frozen Trebia River. Impetuously, and against the advice of Publius Cornelius Scipio, the Roman consul sent his men across the river. Livy would later write:

> . . . without any food, without any protection against the cold, so they had no heat in them and the chilling blasts from the river made the cold still more severe as they approached it in their pursuit of the Numidians. But when they entered the water which had been swollen by the night's rain and was then breast high, their limbs became stiff with cold, and when they emerged on the other side they had hardly strength to hold their weapons; they began to grow faint from fatigue and as the day wore on, from hunger. Hannibal's men, meanwhile, had made fires in front of their tents, oil had been distributed amongst the maniples for them to make their joints and limbs supple and they had time for an ample repast. When it was announced that the enemy had crossed the river they took their arms, feeling alert and active in mind and body, and marched to battle.[154]

The hungry and tired Roman soldiers, many of whom were undoubtedly suffering from hypothermia, reorganized themselves once across the Trebia. Yet their miserable condition allowed the superior generalship of Hannibal to win the day, leading to the almost complete annihilation of the Roman army. Nor were the Carthaginian soldiers exempt from the fury of the winter weather. Many of Hannibal's men also succumbed to the cold, as did almost all of his elephants. Livy recorded that the enemy was "so benumbed with cold that they hardly felt any joy in their victory."[155]

Much as wind helped the rise of Muhammad at the Battle of the Badr Oasis, cold came to his aid at the Battle of the Trench three years later in 627. Outnumbered and surrounded in the city of Medina, Muhammad and his followers dug a series of trenches around the town in order to slow down the cavalry of the Quraysh. Unable to take Medina by direct assault, his enemies settled down to a lengthy siege. According to the Qu'ran, "Remember the favor of Allah towards you when great hosts came against you, and We sent against them a wind and hosts whom you did not see."[156] The desert, while experiencing blistering heat during the day, becomes quite cold at night. The horses, camels, and men of the Quraysh would have suffered immensely from the freezing east wind that descended from the Russian taiga. At the same time, Muhammad's men would have benefited from the urban heat island effect of Medina. After suffering for days, the enemy gave up the siege, not only preserving the freedom of Medina but securing Muhammad in power as well.

One of the other effects of cold weather that could impact battles or campaigns was its ability to freeze rivers. Moving water often served as an instrument of defense, separating armies and protecting castles. Frozen rivers therefore, could afford an opportunity for an army to quickly reach an enemy or allow a trapped foe to escape. The latter case occurred in 1142 in England when the Empress Matilda was able to flee from her castle at Oxford. The town had already fallen weeks before to the forces of Stephen and he had settled down to starve Matilda and her men from the nearly impregnable castle. Just before Christmas, days from having to surrender, the Empress and a handful of her knights fled from the castle across the partially frozen river and made it to Devizes. The Anarchy would continue for another decade in England and Normandy until 1154, when her son Henry I was able to succeed Stephen and secure the throne.

The reverse situation would unfold almost five hundred years later in 1641 when a Franco-Swedish army under Johan Banér almost overran Regensburg in a surprise assault. An imperial Diet was being held in the city in order to restore peace to Germany. Present were the emperor, most of the Roman Catholic rulers in the Electoral College, the majority of bishops, and only a few of the Protestant rulers of Germany. "The Protestants, with reason, considered it a mere combination of Austria and its creature, against their party; and it seemed to them a laudable effort to interrupt its deliberations, and to dissolve the Diet itself."[157] Banér united his Swedish army with a French force under the Comte de Guébriant and launched a surprise attack on Regensburg. Only the breaking up of the previously frozen Danube surrounding the town, thanks to onset of a warm wind, prevented its capture. The Protestant attempt at a coup de main had failed, and the war would drag on for another seven years.

Perhaps no army was more adept at using winter warfare in the ancient world than the Mongols. Whereas other armies would settle down into winter quarters due to lack of available provisions and adverse conditions, the Mongols used the hard, frozen ground to their advantage. More traditional armies, from the ancient Romans to the Germans of World War II, dreaded the frozen ground of winter that prevented them from digging fortifications or entrenchments, yet the horsemen of the Mongolian steppe found that they could cover far greater distances on hard, solid ground. Genghis Khan's descent into China, in fact, was aided by the freezing-over of ordinarily impenetrable marshlands, while in 1241 the great Hungarian city of Esztergom fell to Batu and his cavalry after they were able to race across the frozen Danube.

The Balkans was again the scene of vicious winter fighting against another opponent from the east, this time the Ottoman Turks, in 1443. In a bid to both reverse the advance of the Turks toward Hungary, as well as to relieve pressure on what was left of the Byzantine Empire, King Vladislaus gave John Hunyadi the task of leading a crusade in southeastern Europe. After some initial victories, the onset of a harsh winter brought about the ending of the Long Campaign. What little success was achieved though, convinced many Christian lords to undertake an extensive invasion of Ottoman lands, pushing all the way to Varna on the Black Sea. Unfortunately, the Turks had used the early termination of the Christian offensive the years before to rebuild and reinforce their position in the region. The ensuing battle saw not only the death of Vladislaus but the annihilation of the Christian army. No subsequent help would be sent to relieve the situation in Constantinople and the Byzantine Empire would fall a decade later in 1453, ushering in the Turkish conquest of much of southeastern Europe.

The victory of Parliament during the English Civil War owed as much to the cold of winter as it did the arms of the Roundheads. Timing has always been a key component of warfare and has become more important as time and technology have progressed. The English Civil War was won, in part, by the careful coordination between the Scottish army of the Earl of Leven and an English army under the Earl of Manchester. Alexander Leslie, the Earl of Leven, was able to move quickly south from Scotland in 1644 due to a particularly cold winter. The ice over the Tweed and the Tyne were so thick that both men and equipment were able to march over it without slowing. York came under seige and Leven was able to meet up with Manchester to subsequently deliver a crushing defeat to the Royalists at Marston Moor. Thanks to the frozen rivers, all of Northern England was lost to King Charles and his forces. Parliament moved closer and closer to victory in the war.

King Charles's grandson, James Francis Stuart, also known as the Old Pretender, owed both his defeat and his escape to the cold Scottish winter. When the Pretender landed in Scotland in 1715 he was stricken with an illness that was only worsened by the cold conditions. Unfit to lead effectively, and not finding the local support that he thought he would, Stuart decided to flee the approaching Duke of Argyll. Luckily for him the cold winter had frozen most of the rivers of the country, thus allowing for a quick retreat to the coastline. Stuart sailed to France, setting up his house in exile, which continued to claim to be the rightful heirs to the English throne.

The American Revolution witnessed many episodes of suffering and privation. While the majority of these were caused by disease, the bitter cold of several northern winters also threatened to cut short the existence of the young republic. Emmanuel Leutze's famous painting of Washington crossing the Delaware River, though filled with factual inaccuracies, does highlight one of the problems faced by the Continental Army that night. Though rare today, due to the impact of the Little Ice Age, the Delaware River often froze over during particularly harsh winters. On the night of Washington's crossing, the river contained large sheets of dangerous floating ice. Two of the three attempted crossings, those under Cadwalader and Ewing, failed to reach the battlefield due to the packed ice flows that dominated the river. Luckily for Washington and the American cause, enough men were present to allow for a complete victory at Trenton. The increasing ice on the river actually helped the American soldiers to make another crossing a week later, with many units simply walking across the Delaware. This second incursion led to Continental victories at Assunpink and Princeton and the steady reconquest of New Jersey.

Washington seems to have appreciated the benefits that ice could give to an army a year earlier while he was encamped around Boston. Having surrounded the city and besieged the British inside, the future president had settled upon the decision to await the arrival of artillery from New York to drive out the enemy. Yet a sudden cold snap in mid-February seemed to offer a different strategy.

> The late freezing weather having formed some pretty strong ice from Dorchester Point to Boston Neck, and from Roxbury to the Common, thereby affording a more expanded and consequently a less dangerous approach to the town, I could not help thinking, notwithstanding the militia were not all come in, and we had little or no powder to begin our operation by a regular cannonade and bombardment, that a bold and resolute assault upon the troops in Boston, with such men as we had (for it could not take many men to guard our own lines,

at a time when the enemy were attacked in all quarters), might be crowned with success; and therefore, seeing no certain prospect of a supply of powder on the one hand, and a certain dissolution of the ice on the other, I called the general officers together for their opinion.[158]

Despite his optimism, however, the vast majority of his commanders were not convinced of the efficacy of the plan, and Washington was forced to await the arrival of artillery and reinforcements, which led to the subsequent Battle of Bunker Hill.

The greatest number of casualties during the American Revolution tended to come about in camps rather than on battlefields. This was almost entirely due to disease, which the armies little understood. Nowhere was this truer than at the American winter encampments at Valley Forge in 1777 and Morristown in 1779. Lack of supplies, general privation, filthy conditions, and harsh winter weather led to the deaths of nearly 20 percent of the men at Valley Forge alone. Washington was quick to notify Congress of the dangers faced by his army at Valley Forge, writing in 1777 that "three or four days of bad weather would prove our destruction. What then is to become of the army this winter?"[159] Conditions were so bad in the winter of 1779 that Thomas Matlack, the man who engrossed the final copy of the Declaration of Independence, wrote that, "the ink now freezes in my pen within five feet of the fire in my parlour, at 4 o'clock in the afternoon." Cold and its natural ally of illness was always a greater threat in premodern warfare than the actual enemy.

The American rebels seemed more willing than other armies, perhaps due to their guerrilla nature, to employ winter marches and combat. The epitome of this remains the George Rogers Clark winter campaign of 1779. American frontier soldiers had previously captured Vincennes and several other villages and posts along the Wabash and Illinois Rivers early in the war. Yet, lacking sufficient manpower to hold these positions, they were soon reoccupied by the British under Henry Hamilton. In response, Clark and a body of men undertook a daring wintertime march through the Kentucky and Indiana wilderness to retake Vincennes. Hamilton was taken completely by surprise and the town and its fort was soon once again in American hands. The campaign of Clark helped to secure the Northwest Territory for the new nation and begin its slow conquest of North America.

The French Revolution and subsequent Napoleonic Wars saw a number of radical innovations in the waging of war. The intersection of military necessity and more modern transportation capabilities allowed for at least the beginnings of more consistent winter campaigning. One of the first and most successful involved General Jean-Charles Pichegru's winter offensive in Holland in 1794 and 1795. Thanks to below-freezing temperatures, the French were able to bypass the much-vaunted water defense lines of the Netherlands, which had protected it from invaders for three centuries. After a lightning campaign that lasted two months the Netherlands fell to the French Republic.

Napoleon attempted to repeat the success of the winter campaign in Holland six years later in Northern Italy. As the winter of 1800 approached, the French consul ordered Jacques MacDonald to take his army across the mountains and into Northern Italy in order to eliminate the Austrian presence there. Though some of his subordinates expressed doubt that a crossing could be undertaken so late in the season, Napoleon argued that, "wherever two men could set their feet, an army had the means of passing".[160] Further, the Consul reasoned that freezing terrain was more easily passed than thawing ground.

MacDonald undoubtedly undertook the campaign with a certain amount of foreboding. Feeding into his fears, early on in the march a sudden avalanche killed half of a squadron of dragoons while a snowstorm several days later buried over one hundred men. Cleverly, the Austrian commander in the region had barred the Tonal Pass with a defensive barricade of ice blocks. The bulletproof and readily available material held back two assaults by the French, forcing MacDonald to alter his march. Yet, in the end the persistence of his soldiers would prove Napoleon's tactics. MacDonald descended into the northern Italian plain, driving back the Austrian presence there.

Napoleon's next encounter with cold and ice produced one of the crueler acts of his career. On December 2, 1805, Napoleon crushed a combined Austro-Russian army at the Battle of Austerlitz. As the defeated Russians fled southward, they crossed over a series of frozen ponds. Allegedly, the French emperor ordered his gunners to target the ice rather than the mass of men, cracking the surface of the frozen ponds, and sending many men and horses to an icy death.

Revenge would come several years later during the French invasion of the Russian Empire. Napoleon's push eastward in 1812 would become a cautionary tale of conducting winter warfare in Russia. Even with the more recently established caveat that typhus was a far greater killer of his men then "Generals Janvier and Février," cold and frostbite certainly took their toll as well. A resident of Berlin described the returning French soldiers in haunting terms. "One of them had lost all his ten fingers, another wanted both ears and nose. Still more terrible was the appearance of a third . . . The eyelids hung down rotting, the globes of the eyes were burst."[161] A related factor was the failure of the French to prepare for the shoeing and care for the horses that were so essential to the cavalry, the movement of supplies, and the transportation of artillery. A similar death march was experienced by the British decades later in 1842 as they attempted to evacuate Kabul. Almost the entire force along with women and children were lost to either the guns of the Afghans or the cold and snow of the Hindu Kush.

At the same time halfway around the world a British army was disembarking in Louisiana for an assault on the American port city of New Orleans. Operations in the region had been delayed for almost two years after a massive hurricane in August of 1812 had not only severely damaged the city, but had also crippled much of the British fleet in the Caribbean. While the battle is remembered for a number of interesting reasons, including its taking place after the peace settlement was reached, Andrew Jackson's impressive leadership, the motley crew of assembled civilians that defied the English, and the creative use of cotton bales as improvised defenses, the impact of the weather upon the battle is relatively unknown. Despite British expectations of mild, Southern winter weather, the occurrence of an El Niño during the years 1814 to 1815 produced much colder and wetter weather in the area. With little shelter and sleeping in open areas, the English would have suffered greatly from the freezing temperatures at night. In addition, the two West Indian regiments in the British army would have probably experienced even greater discomfort compared to the other English and local American soldiers.

The alpine crossing experiences of Hannibal and Napoleon have been compared to similar campaigns during the wars of independence in South America. On January 19, 1817, José de San Martín departed with an army of four thousand men and almost ten thousand animals from recently liberated Argentina. His goal was to cross the Andes, an idea thought practically impossible at the time, in order to surprise and defeat royalist forces in Chile. Over the course of a month the Spanish soldiers trekked over the mountains, which even at the height of summer, still tended to be shrouded in snow amid freezing temperatures. As an added precaution, the men brought along large amounts of garlic, which according to folk beliefs would prevent altitude sickness in both men and beasts.[162] In the end, the crossing claimed over one-third of his men and the vast majority of his animals. Though the subsequent Battle of Chacabuco helped to secure the independence of Chile, the loss of only twelve men on the battlefield stands in sharp contrast to the suffering of the army as it crossed the Andes. Simón Bolívar duplicated the feat two years later, crossing the northern branch of the mountains in order to engage and defeat royalist forces at Boyacá, once more losing more men in the crossing from the cold than from battle.

Sometimes though, plummeting temperatures could actually save the lives of soldiers. This proved to be the case in 1862 at the Battle of Shiloh, though the exact reason why was not known for almost 150 years. After an entire day of bloody and bitter fighting in early April at Shiloh, Tennessee, close to twenty thousand casualties littered the area around the battlefield. For the nearly sixteen thousand wounded who lay in the mud, many for up to two days, their chances seemed little better than those who had died outright. As if to add to the horror, many of the wounded found that their bayonet cuts and bullet holes glowed a faint blue-green light at night. The phenomenon became known as the "Angel's Glow" due to the fact that those who exhibited it seemed to actually have a higher rate of survival than those who did not, exhibiting no signs of infection, and healing in a shorter amount of time. Over a century later, two high school students would finally discover that the glow resulted from the presence of the bacterium *Photorhabdus luminescens*. A local species of roundworm, which lives in a symbiotic relationship with the bacteria, expels the bacteria from its gut as it feeds. The bacteria appear to have been attracted to the wounds of the soldiers, destroying and consuming the other developing bacteria there that would have normally led to a slow, painful death for the victim from infection. Though the normal body temperature of the men would have naturally killed off the luminescent bacteria, the cold, early-spring nights in Tennessee had stricken many of the men with hypothermia as they lay in the mud for days. Thanks to the cold, *Photorhabdus luminescens*, more so than the medical service of the Union or Confederacy, saved perhaps thousands of lives at Shiloh.

The World Wars, due to the fact that they were fought year round and in various settings, would see even greater intersections between the element of cold and battle. While the British lost an estimated 115,367 men to cold-related injuries in all theaters during the First World War, the Italian Army suffered three times that number fighting in the Alps alone.[163] The Eastern Front was notoriously plagued by cold weather, as were attempts in 1915 to take the fortified position of Verdun. In response to these conditions, several English companies, most notably Burberry and Aquascutum, helped to produce and popularize light, waterproof coats for use in the trenches. Even with the adoption of these "trench coats" in an effort to reduce hypothermia, the constant immersion of the soldiers' feet in cold, standing water led to an epidemic of debilitating trench foot. The British Army alone reported seventy-five thousand cases in the Western Front.[164] The Americans suffered similar losses during the Aleutian Campaign of World War II, losing almost a third of all casualties due to cold on Attu alone.

In 1915, while attempting to dislodge the Russian Second Army from its position near Bolimow, Poland, the German General August von Mackensen undertook the first use of chemical weapons in the war. To aid in his push toward Warsaw, the German commander authorized the release of xylyl bromide, a tear gas agent, before an assault on the Russian lines. Despite the release of almost twenty thousand chemical-filled shells, freezing temperatures meant that when they exploded, the chemical irritant inside failed to aerosolize, instead raining harmlessly down to the ground. The assault was called off and only the failure of a subsequent Russian counterattack prevented a complete disaster for Berlin.

The Germans experienced as much hardship invading Russia during the Second World War as Napoleon had a century before. Though cold certainly played a role in this, much like with the Grand Army, it was not for the reasons normally associated with it. Hitler and his advisors hoped for a campaign of rapid movement across the western lands of the USSR, repeating both its success in World War I and Subadai's lightning campaign in the same region during the thirteenth century. Cold temperatures would actually help to freeze the Russian roads, which normally were muddy following the rains of October. Unfortunately, the Soviet strategy of withdrawal prolonged the German offensive until weather eliminated one of its primary tools in confronting a communist counterattack. The frozen Russian ground prevented the Germans from being able to dig trenches and foxholes and resist the Soviet human wave attacks that would eventually push them out of Stalingrad and back across the Polish border. Likewise, the equipment fielded by the Germans had not been designed for the weather extremes of western Russia. Stories abound of tank commanders having to light fires under their engines in order to melt frozen oil and gasoline. Ironically, the Russians themselves suffered setbacks due to snow and cold during their Winter War against Finland. The better-trained and lighter-equipped Finns were able to ski over the snowy terrain and transport goods by horseback while the mechanized Soviets who had trained to fight on the open fields of the Ukraine or Poland were at a distinct disadvantage. American units cut off by the Germans at the Bulge faced similar problems, with some groups resorting to dynamite to construct foxholes.[165] Cold temperatures more often hampered defensive operations than offensive ones.

The various Red and White armies of the Russian Civil War had to contend with similar issues from 1917 to 1922. Cold weather hampered movement on both sides, especially during Kornilov's famous Ice March in 1918. During the allied expedition to Northern Russia from 1918 to 1920, the greatest danger faced by the Western nations tended to come from the cold and snow around Archangelsk. A British soldier wrote home complaining that, "sometimes our trousers are frozen on us."[166] Local Bolshevik forces were often better able to utilize the cold to their advantage, such as the Battle of Tulgas where the sudden freezing of swampy ground allowed Russian soldiers to surprise and surround an allied unit. In a similar fashion, American soldiers were stymied in their movement at the Battle of Shenkursk in January of 1919 by waist-deep snow. Nor were the Russians themselves immune to these conditions. During the Battle of Bolshie Ozerki, one Bolshevik unit alone suffered over five hundred casualties from frostbite.

The modern war most associated with the deadly effects of cold remains the Korean War. During the lightning push by United Nations' soldiers north of the 38th parallel, the toughest enemy was not the rapidly dissolving Communist army, but the onset of winter. The extreme cold of northern Korea affected gunpowder, artillery, batteries, and the mechanical components of equipment. Disobeying orders, men would set campfires or simply light pools of gasoline on fire in an effort to keep warm and thaw equipment. In extreme emergencies, the soldiers would simply urinate on frozen weapons in order to make them serviceable.[167] Part of the situation was due to the belief of lawmakers and some in the Pentagon that the war would be over by Christmas, thus appropriate winter gear was not issued to the men in the field. While the rapid initial progress of the American and associated armies northward seemed to validate these forecasts, the onset of cold weather helped to introduce several unplanned-for components into an increasingly complicated war.

Though American leaders and commanders misread Chinese intentions and strength, there were some attempts to reduce the bridges over the Yalu River in order to prevent a possible incursion by Mao. Unfortunately for the allies, these preparations proved moot as the entire river froze over enough to allow the Peoples' Volunteer Army to cross it directly. In the bitter winter fighting that followed, around 90 percent of American soldiers suffered some form of cold injury, specifically frostbite. These numbers are only dwarfed by the 100 percent of men at the Battle of the Chosin Reservoir who were stricken with frostbite. Years later, studies suggest increased rates of skin cancer among those stricken by the cold during the war.[168]

Cold weather in essence has the potential for the same amount of debilitation during war as hot weather. Cold-related injuries, effects on movement and transportation, links to the spreading of disease, and other concerns, all arose from fighting during the winter season. Historically, much of this was avoided due to the propensity of nations not to wage war during winter months. However, due to both necessity and a sense of technological achievement, nations over the past two centuries have resorted to more winter warfare. Though once again this issue is often geographically specific, the presence of mountainous terrain in even a desert country can make cold weather a tactical and strategic concern.

9

OTHER WEATHER CONDITIONS

The earth opened its mouth and swallowed them.
—Numbers 26:10

While some weather phenomena are rarer than others, no study of the impact of this force on war would be complete without their inclusion. Floods, drought, lightning, earthquakes, volcanoes, dust storms, and other natural forces have all played important roles in both battles and campaigns in much the same way as they have in politics, society, and economics. Rarer phenomena are harder to prepare for and thus disproportionately impact battles or campaigns.

FLOOD AND DROUGHT

The debilitating effects of rain, in terms of hampering movement, contributing to the spread of disease, and ruining equipment has already been established. Yet in terms of sheer and immediate destructive power, the impact of rain compares little to the onrush of a sudden flood. It is perhaps not surprising that ancient people from Israel, to Babylon, and as far east as China all employed floods as the weapon of choice by deities for the destruction of humanity. The common concept of the deluge represented the strongest natural force known to most traditional societies.

Both the ancient Hebrews and Indians have similar stories of floods affecting battles. The Biblical narrative of the destruction of Pharaoh's pursuing army by the flooding of the Red Sea shows the suddenness and totality of flooding in combat:

> Then the Lord said to Moses, "Stretch out your hand over the sea, that the waters may come back upon the Egyptians, on their chariots, and on their horsemen." And Moses stretched out his hand over the sea; and when the morning appeared, the sea returned to its full depth, while the Egyptians were fleeing into it. So the Lord overthrew the Egyptians in the midst of the sea. Then the waters returned and covered the chariots, the horsemen, *and* all the army of Pharaoh that came into the sea after them. Not so much as one of them remained.[169]

Likewise, the Rig Veda's account of the Battle of the Ten Kings, said to have taken place during the second millennium BC, depicts the army of King Sudas of the Baharatas winning an important battle over various other Aryan tribes due to the sudden flooding of the Parushni River. In a similar vein to the Biblical tale, Sudas and his men are fleeing before the enemy and are saved only by the intervention of nature and weather. "They parted inexhaustible Paruṣṇī. Lord of the Earth, he with his might repressed them."[170]

Indian history records that King Ajatashatru of Magadha was able to overcome the kingdom of Kosala thanks to a similar turn of events. Though he was at first defeated in his attempts to conquer the region, a sudden flood of the Rapti River appears to have destroyed the Kosalan army around 493 BC, thus allowing Ajatashatru to absorb the kingdom into his own and continue the expansion of Magadha.

Occasionally flooding was not sudden but was nonetheless still destructive in its effects. After battling both cold and snow, Hannibal

managed to cross the Alps and defeat several Roman armies in northern Italy. In order to avoid more enemy armies that could potentially
place him in the same position as King Pyrrhus, Hannibal marched
through Etruria by traversing the Arno marshes. Recent flooding
though had turned the normally impassable marshes into malarial
swamps. Flooded routes and disease claimed many lives and cost the
Carthaginian army equipment, horses, and all but one of its elephants.
Hannibal himself would eventually lose sight in one of his eyes, most
likely to a bacterial or viral infection acquired while crossing the
swamp. Polybius describes the unfortunate Celts in Hannibal's army
as having to sit "upon their dead bodies . . . to get a snatch of sleep."[171]
Much of the Carthaginian general's inability to quickly take Rome or
end the war in the peninsula resulted from his loss of men and matériel
to the flooded fields of the Arno.

Interestingly, most of the occasions when flooding occurred in
combat were due to the intentional efforts of armies and their commanders. The concerted efforts of centuries of farmers and empires to
construct canals and dams in an effort to aid in irrigation made this an
easy task. This was especially desirable in enemy countries where the
secondary effects—famine and pestilence—served as force multipliers.
There are numerous instances of intentional flooding as a defensive
tactic, from the Netherlands to China.

Conversely, the complete absence of water could also negatively impact a battle or campaign. On a micro level this is often
associated with heat and desert warfare and has largely already been
discussed in that chapter. On a macro level drought can direct the
history of nations, producing or inhibiting war. Recent studies suggest the onset of a massive drought that stretched across much of
Eurasia for almost 150 years, ending around 1100 BC.[172] At this time
numerous Bronze Age civilizations, including Egypt, Mycenae, Babylon, Mohenjo-Daro, and the Shang Dynasty, all fell to a marauding
horde known collectively as "the Sea Peoples." While the massive
drought would certainly have weakened these kingdoms internally,

the seminomadic tribes surrounding them would have been more drastically affected. These then pushed into the various kingdoms in order to gain access to the river valleys around which they were built. Thus, extreme drought produced greater conflict, which eventually ushered in the Iron Age.

In a similar way, Europe experienced several years of persistent drought during the last decade of the eleventh century AD. Oppressive conditions, lack of food, and the subsequent rise of famine and pestilence produced a population that was more receptive to the crusading message then being preached by various European leaders. Due to this, not only were Christian leaders able to successfully organize and launch the First Crusade, but also what would become known as the People's Crusade. Peter the Hermit used the appearance of meteors and an eclipse in 1095 to convince a hungry and desperate mass of people to march eastward to the Holy Land. The unprepared and poorly led army was eventually defeated and slaughtered by the Turks at Civetot near Nicaea.

Drought, in a similar way to cold, could help to make once-formidable rivers more fordable to an army. Just such an occurrence helped to ensure the escape of Gen. August V. Kautz and his men toward the end of the ill-fated Wilson-Kautz Raid into Virginia in 1864. After destroying around sixty miles of track, Wilson and Kautz found themselves trapped at the Battle of Ream's Station on June 29, 1864. Luckily, several weeks of heat combined with little to no rainfall to make a nearby swamp passable, thus enabling the escape of both men and the majority of their commands.[173] In fact the hot, dry weather also aided in their primary mission of destroying the railroad lines[174] that fed Lee at Petersburg.[175]

Finally, drought also helped to play a role in the transmittance of disease. As potable water became scarce, soldiers would often turn to stagnant pools or less sanitary sources. Often times, men without access to different and plentiful sources of water would cross-purpose what little they could find for cooking, drinking, bathing, and sanitary needs. Dysentery and other illnesses stalked armies in these circumstances, often times more effectively then the enemy. These conditions confronted the various armies camped at Perryville in Kentucky in 1862. A soldier at the time recounted that they drank "from a pond where men and mules drank fifteen feet apart, across the pond soldiers washed their socks and feet, and at an end of the pond floated a dead mule." The severe drought that gripped Kentucky had in fact been the reason why General William J. Hardee had stopped his wing at Perryville while the rest of Bragg's command had intended to move to Versailles. The water to be had at the town would lead to one of the most important engagements of the war, and with the withdrawal of General Bragg the next day, preserved Kentucky for the Union.

Melting Snow

While heavy snow could slow an army's progress to a crawl as seen in the case of the Greeks of the *Anabasis* and the Americans before Quebec, so too could melting snow. Far from removing an impediment to movement, the rapid melting of a heavy snowfall could turn the ground into a quagmire, preventing movement and trapping heavy vehicles. This was precisely the situation experienced by the German army as it advanced on Moscow in the fall of 1941.

The heavy rains and early, frequently melting snowfalls of the autumn that characterize Eastern Europe gave rise to the term *rasputitsa* to describe the impassable conditions of dirt roads and fields in the area. As the Germans advanced on Moscow, having quickly overcome most previous resistance, they suddenly found themselves bogged down in foot-deep mud that trapped vehicles and slowed their progress. Their once-successful and much-vaunted encirclement campaigns began to fail, and much of the Red Army was able to fall back and prepare defensive lines around the capital. Despite a series of subsequent assaults, the previously unstoppable German juggernaut ground to a halt before Moscow, stymied more by mud than by the bullets of the enemy. Heinz Guderian himself summed up the reason for the defeat as, "We underestimated the enemy's strength, as well as his size and climate."[176]

EARTHQUAKES

Much like comets, many ancient people viewed earthquakes as harbingers of divine wrath or future misfortune. Being such rare and localized events, they did not often affect individual battles. Likewise, casualties from these disasters tended to arise from building collapses and fires, not conditions that would normally predominate an ancient or medieval battlefield. Yet, as with droughts, earthquakes could weaken a nation and invite invasion or set in motion a series of events that could lead to war.

One such case appears to have occurred in Greece in 464 BC. A massive earthquake struck the region of Sparta that year with anecdotal tales describing tens of thousands of deaths and the army being marched from the city to avoid its destruction. Apart from these literary flourishes, what is evident is that the vast slave population of the region used the opportunity to rise up against their Spartan masters. Facing disaster, the Spartans called in their Greek allies to put down the revolt. Athens dutifully sent a large contingent to aid the Lacedaemonians, but the latter, fearing that the Athenians might actually aid the helots, quickly sent them away. The insult caused consternation back in Athens, and the alliance with Sparta was soon in tatters. Years later, the issue was brought up as one of the grievances which set in motion the Peloponnesian War. "Besides, you, as Lacedaemonians, ought not to forget that at the time of the great panic at Sparta, after the earthquake, caused by the secession of the Helots to Ithome, we sent the third part of our citizens to assist you."[177]

Livy mentions at the Battle of Lake Trasimene, "an earthquake, violent enough to overthrow large portions of many of the towns of

Italy, turn swift streams from their courses, carry the sea up into rivers, and bring down mountains with great landslides, was not even felt by any of the combatants."[178] Though the violent event caused no damage to either army, the Roman populace could again look back upon it as a divine portent of disaster. A similar event occurred during the great battle between the Romans and the Huns over six hundred years later at the Catalaunian Fields, though this time with a reversed result.

The view of earthquakes as messages from God persisted even with the rise of Christianity. The Siege of Antioch, undertaken by the knights of the First Crusade, had dragged on for almost six months when in 1098 a massive earthquake struck the region. The chronicler Raymond d'Aguilers recorded the event in the following manner.

> Meanwhile, there was a great earthquake on the third day before the Kalends of January, and we beheld a very marvelous sign in the sky. For in the first watch of the night the sky was so red in the north that it seemed as if dawn had arisen to announce the day. And though in this way God chastised His army, so that we were intent upon the light which was rising in the darkness, yet the minds of some were so blind and abandoned that they were recalled neither from luxury nor robbery. At this time the Bishop prescribed a fast of three days and urged prayers and alms, together with a procession, upon the people; moreover, he commanded the priests to devote themselves to masses and prayers, the clerics to psalms. Thereupon, the merciful Lord, remembering His compassion, put off the punishment of His children, lest the arrogance of their adversaries increase.[179]

The onset of heavy rains only further damped the spirits of both armies and reduced food supplies to a minimum. Only the tenacity of the attackers, the approach of spring, and treachery inside the city finally secured the fall of Antioch.

With the advent of the Scientific Revolution, most modern people began to lose their divine fear of earthquakes, though certainly a practical one remained. Yet for more primitive people, such as the various Native American tribes straddling the Mississippi River in 1811, an earthquake was still viewed as a powerful symbol. As has previously been mentioned, the great Indian chief Tecumseh rose to prominence, in part, due to his ability to seemingly predict comets. His followers sought to bolster his mystical renown still further by claiming that he caused the Great Madrid Earthquake of 1811 as well by simply stomping his foot. Though American settlers along the frontier would not have believed these stories, they were certainly appealing to many Native groups.

One of the few times that an earthquake appears to have actually affected combat occurred during the Israelite conquest of Canaan. According to the Bible, the Israelites under Joshua crossed the Jordan River and laid siege to the town of Jericho. Unable to breach its infamous walls, the Jews were told by God instead to circle the city for seven days blowing horns. On the final day of this display,

> . . . they rose early about the dawning of the day, and compassed the city after the same manner seven times: only on that day they compassed the city seven times. And it came to pass at the seventh time, when the priests blew with the trumpets, Joshua said unto the people, Shout; for the LORD hath given you the city . . . So the people shouted when the priests blew with the trumpets: and it came to pass, when the people heard the sound of the trumpet, and the people shouted with a great shout, that the wall fell down flat, so that the people went up into the city, every man straight before him, and they took the city.[180]

Frequent seismic activities in the region could easily explain the fortuitous collapse of the wall before the Israelites. While recent archaeological evidence does show collapsed walls and fire dating to roughly the time of the Jewish migration, it is also possible that it fell just before their arrival. Either way, with the collapse of Jericho's famed walls, the plains of Canaan were open to Jewish expansion.

Volcanoes

Much like droughts, volcanoes rarely if ever directly affected the battlefield. Instead, their impact on cities or nations could invite invasion
or alter the geopolitical landscape. It has been postulated that the massive volcanic explosion at Thera in the Mediterranean around 1530 BC
led to the collapse of numerous world civilizations. Included among
these would be the local Minoans and Mycenaeans, the Xia, and the
Hyksos, who had invaded the Nile Delta. Some historians have proposed that the Hittite raid that destroyed Babylon in 1531 BC led by
Mursili I was in response to food shortages caused by the volcano and
its associated effect on the climate.[181]

In a similar vein, the eruption of Krakatoa in Indonesia in the year 535
AD possibly ushered in a dramatic series of climate changes that affected
large parts of the world. Several scholars have speculated that the event
is connected to the decline of Teotihuacan and the Moche people in the
Americas as well as the outbreak of the Justinian Plague. Other volcanic results tended to be much more minor, such as an eruption of Vesu-
vius in 1944, which destroyed eighty-eight American B-25 bombers stationed at an airbase nearby. The event caused the USS *Philadelphia* to raise
anchor and sail quickly away, the only time "she turned stern to a foe."[182]

Dust Storms

Dust storms combine many of the worst elements of other weather
phenomenon. One of the more famous anecdotes connecting it to
war occurred in the reign of King Cambyses II of Persia. Having conquered most of Egypt, the Persian leader sent an army westward to the
famed Oracle of Amun at the Siwa Oasis amidst the deserts of eastern
Libya. As recorded by Herodotus:

> Thus far the army is known to have made its way; but thenceforth
> nothing is to be heard of them . . . That the Persians set forth from
> Oasis across the sand, and had reached about half way between that

place and themselves when, as they were at their midday meal, a wind arose from the south, strong and deadly, bringing with it vast columns of whirling sand, which entirely covered up the troops and caused them wholly to disappear.[183]

Finding the Lost Army of Cambyses became a legendary obsession of many kings and archaeologists.

In the early part of the seventh century, Arab armies were subduing large swaths of the Middle East. Even the combined might of the Byzantine and Persian armies proved unable to halt this determined advance. A Muslim army camped in July of 636 at the village of al-Qadisiyyah near the Euphrates River attempted to convert the Persians to Islam and peacefully annex the region. Following a breakdown in talks and the lessening of tensions in Syria, the Arab armies prepared for battle. The resulting engagement resulted in a crushing defeat for the Persian forces and ushered in the collapse of the Sassanid dynasty. Perhaps the greatest loss for the Persians however, was the death of their commander Rostam Farrokhzād. At some point on the last day of battle, a sandstorm struck the region. While sources vary as to the exact moment of his demise, Rostam was killed in the confusion that followed, demoralizing his soldiers and leading to their final, disorganized withdrawal from the battlefield.[184]

Nearly a millennium and a half later, a series of dust storms led to the loss of a much smaller force as well. A rescue attempt launched by President Carter during the Iran Hostage Crisis in 1980 ended in failure due to dust storms, haboobs, sand conditions, and a series of tragic events. Five of the eight aircraft involved in the attempt were either damaged or destroyed with severe loss of life. The mission was a failure and helped to contribute to Carter's election loss that year. Minor amounts of dust, either thrown up by winds or by an army itself could also impact a battlefield. According to Plutarch:

For a great dust being raised, which (as it might very probably happen) almost covered both the armies, he, leading on his forces to the pursuit, missed the enemy, and having passed by their array, moved for a good space, up and down the field; meanwhile the enemy, by chance, engaged with Catulus . . . The dust, too, gave the Romans no small addition to their courage, inasmuch as it hid the enemy. For afar off they could not discover their number; but every one advancing to encounter those that were nearest to them, came to fight hand to hand before the sight of so vast a multitude had struck terror into them. They were so much used to labour, and so well exercised, that in all the heat and toil of the encounter, not one of them was observed either to sweat or to be out of breath; so much so, that Catulus himself, they say, recorded it in commendation of his soldiers.[185]

The most impactful dust storm of modern warfare remains the haboob that struck coalition forces in Iraq from March 25–27 in 2003. Adverse dust and cloud conditions during the Persian Gulf War in 1991 led to the cancellation of nearly 25 percent of all flights by F-117s as well as over three hundred sorties in one day alone.[186] Though lessons from the Gulf War had resulted in changes to weapon systems, weather forecasting, and information sharing, the American military turned out to be ill-prepared for the massive dust storm that struck as they advanced on Baghdad. Striking only five days after the start of the invasion, the storm slowed most units to a crawl and threatened to delay the planned lightning advance on Baghdad. The storm likewise impacted air operations, with the carriers *Kitty Hawk, Abraham Lincoln,* and *Constellation* losing 20 percent of their capability.[187] Luckily for the coalition forces, the storm was short-lived and the campaign was able to proceed.

NEAP TIDES

Tides are a regular phenomenon, and though early man may not have understood the origin of the phenomenon, its timing soon became apparent. Yet, tide little impacted most of military history. Naval battles tended to be fought in the open ocean and land combat was usually far removed from the beach. At best, attacks on coastal fortifications, like that undertaken by Rear Admiral David Farragut at Mobile Bay in 1864, had to deal with water depth issues as ships became larger and heavier.

With the advent of amphibious warfare, however, tides became an important factor in the planning of campaigns and battles. It was at this point that small variations in the normal consistency of tides could prove to be nearly disastrous. The island of Tarawa was considered necessary in 1943 for the eventual conquest of the Mariana Islands. Therefore fifty-three thousand American soldiers launched an offensive to clear the roughly Japanese garrison of approximately twenty-six hundred men from the atoll. Despite careful planning for weather and terrain conditions, and perceived adequate planning for the impact of the tide on the landing craft, a rare tidal event nearly ruined the entire operation.

Neap tides occur shortly after the first and third quarters of the moon, when the sun and moon are at right angles to the Earth. The resulting tide stays relatively flat, with little difference between high and low tide. One such event occurred just as the Marines were attempting to bypass the coral reef that surrounded Tarawa. The normally five feet of water that flowed over the reef at high tide would have allowed the units to land with little difficulty. Unfortunately, the unanticipated neap tide prevented the American Higgins boats from making it over the reef and seriously complicated the assault. In the end, sheer numbers and the tenacity of the troops turned the potential rout into an Allied victory, though at the cost of almost thirty-eight hundred casualties on the American side.

THUNDER AND LIGHTNING

Of all of the weapons assigned to the gods by early cultures, lightning remained the most popular. Zeus remains probably the best-known deity who possessed and used lightning to most Westerners, famously using it to put down the revolt of the titans and secure his throne on Mt. Olympus. Other notable lightning-armed gods include Marduk of Babylon, Ba'al, Set, Thor, and Chaac. Perhaps not surprisingly, almost all were the chief gods of their respective religions as well.

With the exception of the Trojan War, no campaign to the Greeks was more visited by divine intervention than the Gallic attack on Delphi in 279 BC. As the center of Apollonian worship and as the home of the most famous oracle in Greece, the inhabitants of the area usually regarded the town with a high degree of respect. The sanctity of the area was shattered though in 279 BC, when a massive Gallic army under Brennus descended into the Greek peninsula. Centuries of gifts to the oracle stored at the temples there proved to be an inviting target. The various Greek states had suffered from centuries of warfare, foreign invasion, and most recently the conquests of Macedonia and struggled to contain this newest onslaught. Various ancient writers attributed the subsequent Hellenic victory to the intercession of the gods. Not surprisingly this took place through natural phenomenon.

Pausanias, whose theory is the most plausible, states that, "soon portents boding no good to the barbarians were sent by the god, the clearest recorded in history. For the whole ground occupied by the Gallic army was shaken violently most of the day, with continuous thunder and lightning."[188] The sound and fury of the lightning storm limited the ability of the invading army to move or communicate and certainly spread fear and terror among the men of Brennus. Justinus, who wrote an epitome to Pompeius Trogus's *Philippic Histories*, claimed that an earthquake triggered by the gods saved the Greeks. "For a part of the mountain, broken off by an earthquake, overwhelmed a host of the Gauls and some of the densest bodies of the enemy were scattered abroad, not without wounds, and fell to the earth."[189] Either portent was seen as divinely influenced, especially considering the sacred nature of the location.

Another peculiarity of lightning was that it could affect individuals as well as large armies. Numerous noteworthy people, such as James

Otis, Georg Wilhelm Richmann, and possibly Romulus, were all killed by lightning strikes. In terms of famous generals killed by lightning, the most noteworthy would be Gnaeus Pompeius Strabo. Around the year 87 BC, while fighting against Cinna during the Civil War of Sulla, a lightning strike killed Strabo near Rome.

Thunder was often less of a nuisance in combat than rain, though the combined effect of both was certainly more deleterious than either was individually. Other notable battles that experienced these conditions included the Battle of Marston Moor in 1644, the Siege of Genoa in 1800, the Battle of Teugen-Hausen in 1809, and the Battle of Salamanca in 1812. The latter in fact saw a number of casualties when a lightning bolt struck amidst the Fifth Dragoon Guards.

Good Weather

Oftentimes the absence of weather was as important as its presence. Just as the onset of snow, rain, or cold could impact a battle or campaign, so too could the arrival of calm weather. This would especially be noticeable if it arrived either immediately following a more drastic system of weather or at a time of year that normally witnessed much harsher storms and conditions.

A prime example of this was Cyrus the Great's conquest of Assyria during the sixth century BC. The Greek writer Xenophon in his treatise on Cyrus recorded that, "We drew nearer and nearer to the foe, until only four miles separated us. We'd been blessed with good weather during the march into Assyria, and even now no rain fell to trouble us."[190] Undoubtedly, ancient rulers, much like their modern counterparts, overplanned for campaigns knowing that a fair amount of men and matériel would be lost to disease and weather. Thus, Cyrus's good fortune in having pleasant weather during his march would have allowed him to bring even greater numbers to bear against the enemy, all but assuring his victory.

A more recent example involves the last days of the Battle of the Bulge. As has already been discussed, cold and snow were taking their toll on the Allied units stranded around Bastogne. Facing a potential disaster, while Eisenhower and others scrambled to discuss their options, General Patton had Monsignor James Hugh O'Neill type up a prayer to God for more favorable weather for distribution to every man under his command:

> Almighty and most merciful Father, we humbly beseech Thee, of Thy great goodness, to restrain these immoderate rains with which we have had to contend. Grant us fair weather for Battle. Graciously hearken to us as soldiers who call upon Thee that, armed with Thy power, we may advance from victory to victory and crush the oppression and wickedness of our enemies, and establish Thy justice among men and nations. Amen.

Almost miraculously the weather over France cleared the next day and allowed Patton to push his army toward Bastogne. The last German lines collapsed shortly after Christmas and the march toward Berlin continued. For his part in helping to save the American army, Patton subsequently awarded O'Neill with a Bronze Star.

The clearing of weather over the Ardennes was perhaps fitting, since the war had started under similar conditions. The German invasion of Poland in 1939 was visited by unseasonably mild and dry weather in Eastern Europe. Many of the great rivers of Poland, such as the Vistula, which would have normally served as formidable barriers to the Nazis, were instead easily crossable. This allowed for an even quicker conquest of Poland than even the Germans had predicted.

Weather and natural phenomenona are related in the sense that they were often unpredictable in warfare and imposing in the amount of devastation they could cause. Impacting movement, ruining equipment, helping to spread disease, devastating plans, and producing death in and of themselves, these natural conditions proved to be one of the most important, and at the same time usually uncontrollable, elements in military history.

10

WEATHER AS A WEAPON

*Bill grabbed that cyclone by the ears and pulled himself
onto her back. Then he let out a whoop and headed that
twister across Texas.*
—James Cloyd Bowman, *Pecos Bill:
The Greatest Cowboy of All Time*

Religion arose among early men partially in an attempt to explain
natural phenomena and partially in an attempt to control them. Out
of all of these natural conditions, disease and weather stood out as the
most important, most devastating, and, in the case of weather especially, most necessary to understand in order to build agricultural societies. Weather has obviously played an important role in the history of
warfare as well, pushing nations to war, influencing battle, and deciding winners. It appears that early man quickly found ways to utilize
disease in combat, sending sick soldiers into enemy camps or distrib-
uting items that were thought to carry infection. An investigation of
the historical record will show that commanders have also attempted
to harness and use nature in the same way.

Perhaps the most obvious examples involve the beseeching of
gods for good weather, or conversely to send storms upon the enemy.
Various ancient texts include such episodes, from Elijah praying for

rain to show the power of God to King Ahab, to Odysseus's constant battles with and pleas to the gods for good weather on his long voyage home. Yet this is far from an extinct practice. As has been discussed in a previous chapter, Patton's concern with the weather preventing him from relieving trapped American units at Bastogne compelled him to turn to prayer. However, more frequently military leaders have historically sought to find creative ways to employ weather themselves, rather than relying on simple divine intervention.

The destructive power of rain and subsequent flooding was one of the easiest for early man to both understand and control. Numerous examples exist of commanders who have attempted to divert waterways in order to inundate an opponent. Perhaps the first recorded case occurred around 1732 BC in Mesopotamia. King Abi-Eshuh of Babylon, the grandson of Hammurabi, attempted to push Ilum-ma-ili, the founder of the Sealand Dynasty, out of southern Sumer. In order to do this, he dammed the Tigris River so that the swampy region being used by Ilum-ma-ili to hide his army would become dry and exposed.

Over a thousand years later, Cyrus the Great of Persia would perform a similar feat in order to capture the city of Babylon. Protected on all sides by massive fortifications, its only weak point was the Euphrates River, which flowed through the walls and the town. According to Herodotus:

> Cyrus was now reduced to great perplexity, as time went on and he made no progress against the place. In this distress either someone made the suggestion to him, or he bethought himself of a plan, which he proceeded to put in execution. He placed a portion of his army at the point where the river enters the city, and another body at the back of the place where it issues forth, with orders to march into the town by the bed of the stream, as soon as the water became shallow enough: he then himself drew off with the unwarlike portion of his host, and made for the place where Nitocris dug the basin for the river, where he did exactly what she had done formerly: he turned

the Euphrates by a canal into the basin, which was then a marsh, on which the river sank to such an extent that the natural bed of the stream became fordable.

Hereupon the Persians who had been left for the purpose at Babylon by the river-side, entered the stream, which had now sunk so as to reach about midway up a man's thigh, and thus got into the town. Had the Babylonians been apprised of what Cyrus was about, or had they noticed their danger, they would never have allowed the Persians to enter the city, but would have destroyed them utterly; for they would have made fast all the street gates which gave access to the river, and mounting upon the walls along both sides of the stream, would so have caught the enemy, as it were, in a trap. But, as it was, the Persians came upon them by surprise and so took the city. Owing to the vast size of the place, the inhabitants of the central parts (as the residents at Babylon declare) long after the outer portions of the town were taken, knew nothing of what had chanced, but as they were engaged in a festival, continued dancing and reveling until they learnt about the capture. Such, then, were the circumstances of the first taking of Babylon.[191]

King Agis II of Sparta devised a cleverer use of flooding during the latter half of the Peloponnesian War. Faced with a larger Argive and Athenian army that had dug into the hills above Mantinea, the Spartan leader was convinced of the need to lure the enemy down into the plain where the superior Spartan army would decimate it. Thucydides recorded that in order to accomplish this:

> He marched back into the district of Tegea, and proceeded to turn the water into the Mantinean territory. This water is a constant source of war between the Mantineans and Tegeans, on account of the great harm which is done to one or other of them according to the direction which the stream takes. Agis hoped that the Argives and their allies when they heard of this movement would come down from the

hill and try to prevent it; he could then fight them on level ground. Accordingly he stayed about the water during the whole day, diverting the stream. Now the Argives and their confederates were at first amazed at the sudden retreat of their enemies when they were so near, and did not know what to think . . . soon they quitted the hill, and advancing into the plain took up a position with the intention of attacking.[192]

The Spartan ploy worked. The Argive/Athenian army was subsequently defeated after a particularly heavy battle, its leader was killed, and Sparta was able to drive the enemy from its lands.

Wind and currents were another natural phenomenon that man eventually realized he could control or at least utilize in war. As has already been discussed, Datis most likely sought to rely on the Etesian winds to outpace the Athenian army after Marathon and reach their capital first. During the next Persian war, inspired by the Oracle at Delphi who prophesized that they should, "pray for the winds; for the winds would do Greece good service," the Greeks did just that prior to the Battle of Artemisium. Subsequently a powerful wind did erupt which helped to devastate the Persian fleet. Perhaps not willing to rely on the fickle gods again, the Greeks chose the bay by Salamis for their next naval engagement against the enemy, realizing that their heavier ships would be more steady against the winds and currents in the narrow confines of those waters.

The Roman general Marcus Furius Camillus was named dictator five times over the course of his life in order to save Rome from various perilous episodes. One of these times was in 389 BC when the Latin tribes, the Aequi, and the Volsci attacked Roman territory. The enemy was camped securely behind a stout wooden palisade on a hillside. Rather than assault it directly, Camillus decided upon a fire attack to reduce the walls, an attack whose effect would be augmented by the use of nature. Plutarch recounts the dictator's use of nature in the following . . .

Camillus . . . finding their rampart was all of timber, and observing that a strong wind constantly at sun-rising blew off from the mountains, after having prepared a quantity of combustibles, about break of day he drew forth his forces, commanding a part with their missiles to assault the enemy with noise and shouting on the other quarter, whilst he, with those that were to fling in the fire, went to that side of the enemy's camp to which the wind usually blew, and there waited his opportunity. When the skirmish was begun, and the sun risen, and a strong wind set in from the mountains, he gave the signal of onset; and heaving in an infinite quantity of fiery matter, filled all their rampart with it, so that the flame being fed by the close timber and wooden palisades, went on and spread into all quarters. The Latins, having nothing ready to keep it off or extinguish it, when the camp was now almost full of fire, were driven back within a very small compass, and at last forced by necessity to come into their enemy's hands, who stood before the works ready armed and prepared to receive them; of these very few escaped, while those that stayed in the camp were all a prey to the fire, until the Romans, to gain the pillage, extinguished it.[193]

Careful observation of wind patterns had delivered victory into the hands of Camillus.

Another dictator, Gaius Marius, devised a similarly effective use of nature several centuries later. Apart from the aforementioned dust and heat that confronted the Cimbri as they engaged the Romans at the Battle of Vercellae in 101 BC, Marius also sought to use the sun as an ally. The Roman general chose his position carefully in order to have the "sun that shone in the faces of the Cimbri . . . and were much out of breath, being forced to hold their shields before their faces."[194]

Astrologers and astronomers remained components of both governments and militaries around the world well into the second millennium. They served to not only predict future victory and events, but also explain away bad omens. As has been previously seen, astral events such as eclipses and comets were among the most feared of natural portents. Therefore, the ability to accurately predict the movement of the heavenly bodies and the arrival of various events was of high importance to ancient and medieval monarchs. Various monarchs of the Tang Dynasty in China sought to mitigate the problem of unexpected celestial phenomena by employing the astronomer Yi Xing in the early part of the eighth century. The empire's long history of quasi-religious agrarian rebellions overthrowing dynasties necessitated proper understanding of the phenomena that were often used to rally the peasants to a revolt. As late as World War II, the Nazis employed Karl Ernst Krafft in an attempt to both predict future events through his readings of the heavens as well as to provide propaganda to support the war effort. Not to be outdone, the British MI5 hired Louis de Wohl as an astrologer to counter the Nazis.

Often the successful commander is the one who discovers the weakness of the enemy and exploits it. This was exactly the case at various points during the Crusades where Muslim generals used the heat and drought of the region that so thoroughly plagued European armies, to their advantage. As has been previously described, Saladin managed to draw the army of Guy of Lusignan away from his secure and well-watered camp at Sephorie and march into the much drier region of Hattin. Guy's daytime march dehydrated his men, a weakness that Saladin decided to exploit further. His men proceeded to set fire to the high grass surrounding the Crusader's camp, adding smoke to the air and further drying out the throats of the enemy. The resulting disaster at the Horns of Hattin served as a lesson to Richard the Lionheart, who during his march toward Jerusalem in 1191 wisely chose to stay near the coast and move during only the cooler hours of the day.

The Spanish attempted a similar action during the English campaign against Cartagena in 1741. As part of the War of Jenkin's Ear, Admiral Edward Vernon sailed a large force of over 180 ships and 23,000 men to the coast of modern-day Colombia. Blas de Lezo, the Spanish commander, realized that though he was heavily outnumbered he could rely on two natural forces to aid him in his fight against the British: Rain and disease. Though the Spanish were unaware of the actual scientific connection between the two, de Lezo orchestrated a fighting withdrawal in order to delay the English campaign until the onset of the rainy season. Weather would then further slow down Vernon and buy time for the more important ally of the Spanish, Yellow Fever. The longer the English soldiers spent in crowded, wet conditions in the region, the more that pestilence decimated their forces. Finally, by May of 1741 with around ten thousand deaths, mostly from disease, and seven thousand more men wounded or sick, Vernon decided to withdraw.

Sometimes battles were determined by an army's decision to not utilize the advantages that weather gave them. In 1526 a massive Ottoman army, complete with an impressive train of artillery, wound its way over the Balkan Mountains and advanced toward the valley of Mohacs. The Hungarian army of Louis II watched as the Turks struggled to pass the marshy terrain, made worse by rains, and assemble their army on some nearby hills. While some commentators have suggested that it was the Hungarians' belief in chivalry which prevented them from attacking an unformed opponent, dissent and disunion within the command of Louis II may also have played a role. Regardless, the Hungarians lost a vital opportunity to defeat their scattered enemy and were instead cut down in a foolish charge against their larger opponent. Mohacs would spell the end of the Hungarian kingdom and usher in Turkish dominance for centuries.

Inundation by water continued to be a favorite weapon of generals and conquerors. Hulagu Khan, the grandson of Genghis, utilized just such a tactic in 1258 during his campaign against the Abbasid capital at Baghdad. After the Mongols had finally drawn the main Arab army out of the city for battle, Hulagu sent a small force to shatter the irrigation works on the Tigris. Not only was the enemy defeated, but they became trapped between the Mongol army and the now overflowed river. The flower of the Abbasid army was slaughtered and the way was paved for Hulagu's subsequent siege and conquest of Baghdad, the destruction of which permanently scared the surrounding region for the next seven hundred years. As late as 1943, British bombers taking part in Operation Chastise employed bouncing bombs to breach the Mohne and Edersee Dams in attempts to flood the Ruhr Valley and produce similar death and destruction.

Sometimes a nation would choose to flood itself to provide natural defensive works against a more powerful foe. Unfortunately, flooding can often be unpredictable and its long-term effects can dwarf any immediate defensive benefit. William of Orange tried just such a strategy during the Eighty Years' War against the Spanish. At various points, the Dutch commander flooded areas around Antwerp, Ghent, and Bruges. Yet, not only were the Spanish able to secure all three locations, but the inundation by seawater served to devastate the soil quality and therefore farming in the region for centuries. A repetition of these acts by the retreating Germans in 1944 only further added to the misery of the region. Likewise, the Germans attempted to re-flood land south of Rome that had been reclaimed by Mussolini in a move to reintroduce disease-carrying mosquitos. It was hoped that these natural biological weapons would cripple the Allied advance up the peninsula.

The Soviets attempted the same tactic on a much larger scale in 1941 as the Germans approached the capital city of Moscow. Soviet General Headquarters ordered various dams destroyed not merely to flood the region, but also to break up the ice on the Volga River and thus prevent an easy crossing for the Germans. Perhaps the most tragic example of this however, was the decision by the retreating Chinese army in 1938 to break the dykes alongside the Yellow River in an attempt to slow down the advancing Japanese. In the end, close to five hundred thousand people were killed, millions more were affected, and the operation did little to halt the enemy's advance toward Wuhan.

Commanders have even manipulated the usually taboo campaign season of winter with its associated ice and snow to their advantage. During the early days of the American Revolution, General Washington found himself facing an entrenched British adversary in Boston with little to no artillery support. A small colonial force had captured the English fort at Ticonderoga on May 10, 1775, along with its large cache of cannons and gunpowder. It quickly became apparent to Washington and others that if these could be brought to bear against Boston, the subsequent evacuation of the British would clear all royal troops from the Thirteen Colonies. Henry Knox executed the assignment, and by utilizing sleds over the snow-covered countryside and by having his men use water in an attempt to thicken preexisting ice, he was eventually able to complete the journey and deliver the artillery to Washington at Boston. Although the snow impeded his movement as much as it helped him, Knox was not only able to complete his assignment but demonstrated that it was possible to beat a season or weather phenomenon, or to use it to advantage.

French soldiers also employed snow in 1808 to capture the fortified city of Pamplona. Napoleon had launched a series of surprise assaults on a number of key Spanish cities in February of that year in an attempt to conquer northeastern Iberia. The soldiers assigned to the task of taking Pamplona, when denied access to the town by its garrison, proceeded instead to launch a snowball fight. The bemused guards, thinking it a friendly game, rushed out to "fight" the French. Once outside the walls, the French drew their weapons and seized the guards and subsequently the town. "The most important fortress in north-central Spain had fallen to a handful of French soldiers armed with snowballs."[195]

As previously seen, fog could prove to be an important factor in battle if it could be controlled and therefore used to cover an army's advance or retreat. The closest man has come to such an accomplishment historically has been the use of smoke and dust. A Swedish army under Charles XII employed burning ships to mask their successful crossing of the Duna River near Riga in 1701. The natural output of steam engines at sea became a convenient method by which to produce a smokescreen. Confederate blockade runners during the American Civil War became notorious for using this tactic. Unfortunately, unfavorable winds could easily upset these attempts, as during the British raid on Zeebrugge in 1918. On land the tactic could be accomplished most effectively through the use of horses to kick up dust, smoke-producing machines, or the release of opaque gases. The latter were first used on a large scale in WWI and continued to appear in later conflicts as well.

Campaigning in the Middle East in the twentieth century brought with it the ancient enemy of heat. Yet, with modern technology and transportation networks, much of the effects of this could be reduced or prevented. During the British campaign against Ramadi in 1917, around 127 trucks and vans were utilized to transport ice to the battlefield daily in order to keep the men cool and avoid heatstroke. Even with this precaution it would take two battles before the English were finally able to break through.

Overall, if World War I can be called the war of the chemist and the laboratory, World War II was the war of the meteorologist. Almost all major operations and campaigns launched during the war included as part of their operation planning a study of local weather patterns. To undertake this, both sides began setting up weather ships in the Atlantic as early as 1940. The Allies clearly had an advantage in this due to the fact that weather fronts moved from west to east across Europe, therefore necessitating missions by the Germans to set up vessels in inaccessible and hostile Allied waters. Unfortunately for the Nazis, the allies sank or captured almost all of their weather ships. Worse yet, the captured weather ship *Lauenburg* provided the Allies with the much-desired Enigma code books and machine parts. Yet that is not to say that the Allies did not suffer losses as well. In September of 1942, the Coast Guard ship *Muskeget* was torpedoed and sunk by a German U-boat while relaying weather information in the North Atlantic; all men aboard were lost.

The competition to establish more permanent bases would send German and Allied units to distant Arctic islands and challenge the ability of nations to remain neutral in the conflict. As the Germans moved to establish weather stations in Spitsbergen and other places after their invasion of Norway, the English government decided on the radical step of occupying then-neutral Iceland. Though nominally a possession of Denmark, the island had declared its neutrality in the conflict after the fall of Copenhagen. Churchill and others felt that the potential seizure of the island by the Germans to use for air, naval, and meteorological efforts necessitated this invasion. The next year the Allies launched Operation Gauntlet, which aimed at raiding Spitsbergen and destroying German weather equipment there. Though Free Norwegian troops established a presence in 1942, the Nazis returned in 1943 as part of Operation Zitronella. In fact German soldiers on the island were some of the last to surrender in the war. Being so cut off from Berlin they held on until September of 1945 before finally laying down their arms. Further afield the Germans set up four weather stations on the eastern coast of Greenland, which local and American soldiers took years to eradicate. Perhaps most interestingly, an Axis sub landed in Labrador and set up Weather Station Kurt in 1944. This automated system was so well camouflaged that it was not discovered until 1977.

Von Rundstedt once stated that, "Weather was a weapon the German army used with success." From the invasion of Poland set to coincide with dry weather before autumn, to the delay of its offensive against the Allies at Bastogne until sufficient fog and snow had accumulated, Berlin showed time and time again the value of coordinating campaigns with nature. The Allies though, were also heavily reliant upon weather forecasts. Perhaps none was more infamous than Captain James Stagg's forecast, which led General Eisenhower to delay the Normandy landings until June 6. The Japanese also sought to use nature to their advantage, sending balloon bombs on the recently discovered Jet Stream across the Pacific in hopes of causing damage to the American homeland.

Modern science has made planning for the proper use of weather far easier. Professional meteorological services are now associated with practically every military on the planet. As noted previously, the United States Air Force developed the Air Weather Service in the 1960s to track solar storms and flares.[196] In fact, science has advanced far enough to allow man to influence weather itself and direct it to an extent. In Vietnam the US military used various methods to combat fog and create rain. During the communist offensive against Khe Sanh as part of Tet, C-123 airplanes dropped salt on ground fog in order to help disperse it. Likewise, the Air Force took part in rainmaking and cloud seeding over Laos and Cambodia in 1967 and 1968 in order to flood regions, create mud, and generally slow down movement on the Ho Chi Minh Trail. Likewise, Nixon considered the use of nuclear weapons to breach dams along the Red River in 1969 as part of Operation Duck Hook. This would have flooded must of the North's industrial heartland and caused untold devastation.

In the 1990s, Saddam Hussein became adept at using various forms of weather and nature in order to defeat his opponents and avoid his own destruction. During the Persian Gulf War, he famously lit the oil wells of Kuwait on fire not only as a rearguard revenge action, but also to produce acrid black smoke and to hinder the bombing missions of Allied aircraft. Following the conflict, he infamously drained the vast Mesopotamian Marshes around Basra to drive out the local population and to remove hiding places for rebel groups. Finally, he constructed dams in the northern section of the country in order to flood regions inhabited by the Kurds.

Part of the adjustment to fighting in different climates and weather extremes has been the proper incorporation of clothing and equipment. As early as the eighth century BC, Assyrian soldiers were wearing leather boots in order to protect their feet from the elements. They were often reinforced with pieces of metal around the shin and had nails on the sole for better traction. The majority of other ancient warriors went into combat only wearing sandals, though the Romans did incorporate the nail concept as well.[197] From 1801 to 1812, the British developed a very effective "great coat" to protect their soldiers in northern climes against the harshness of winter warfare.

Similarly, the nineteenth and twentieth centuries saw an increase in the use of camouflage in order to help soldiers blend into different terrains. The Germans famously employed white parkas to help them blend in during winter operations, especially during the Battle of the Bulge, a practice that was previously utilized by the Austrians in the Italian Alps during World War I. Allied troops quickly responded by covering their helmets with white lace and bedsheets given to them by grateful local civilians in order to blend in while in their foxholes.[198] Japanese members of Unit 731 tested various cold conditions on prisoners of war in order to learn how to better treat frostbite conditions.

Weather, if properly exploited, could also be a valuable ally to an outnumbered opponent. The island of Malta had always been a valuable, strategic location for control of the central Mediterranean. Due to this it became the scene of a heated campaign by the Axis powers in 1941 and 1942 to drive the British from the region. On March 22, 1942, as an Italian naval force and invasion fleet sailed toward Malta, a much smaller British unit intended to rely upon luck and weather to counter their numerical inferiority. A steadily blowing southeast wind allowed the British ships to run smoke and lessen the impact of the Italian guns. The British were able to hold out against the enemy until nearly sunset when the winds changed and a large storm blew into the area. Fearing torpedo attack and the effects of the tempest, the Italians withdrew from the area.

Numerous Western governments experimented with weather modification techniques starting shortly after World War II. One of the earliest was Project Cirrus, which dropped 180 pounds of dry ice into the eye of a hurricane that was heading away from the Atlantic Seaboard. Though the experiment was initially proclaimed a success, the storm then suddenly changed course, making landfall near Savannah, Georgia. The destruction was subsequently blamed on the government's intervention, and the project was soon cancelled. Operation

Stormfury, which continued throughout the 1960s and into the 1970s, had some measure of success in weakening storms but was eventually cancelled by the Navy. The Russians and British also experimented with cloud seeding, hail control, and numerous other types of weather modification. Secretary of Defense William S. Cohen mentioned speculation about weather experimentation at a conference on terrorism in 1997: "Others are engaging even in an eco-type of terrorism whereby they can alter the climate, set off earthquakes, volcanoes remotely through the use of electromagnetic waves."[199]

Finally, the various heavenly bodies themselves have not escaped the realm of use as potential weapon platforms. In the 1950s talk abounded about locating nuclear missile launchers on the surface of the moon as a backup system should the Russians launch a first strike against the United States. As part of this, the American government formed Project A-119 in 1958, which was aimed at detonating a nuclear device on the surface of the moon itself. Leonar Reiffel, the project's leader, later stated that the purpose was scientific, military, and political. "Concerning the capability of nuclear weapons for space warfare . . . (including) discussion of the moon as military high ground."[200] Due to fears of the public backlash should the project fail, senior leaders subsequently cancelled A-119. Yet interest in weaponizing space with nuclear bombs and asteroid-like kinetic weapons appeared once more with Reagan's Star Wars proposal and various other projects by both Russia and China in the late twentieth and early twenty-first centuries.

The ability to control weather through prayer and divination has remained a constant, though of declining influence, in human history. Conversely, attempts to imitate and resist weather phenomena have only increased. Perhaps the most telling sign remains tales of earthquake bombs and typhoon machines that various governments have sought to produce over the past fifty years. An army that could control the most destructive aspects of nature would not only possess tremendous power, but plausible deniability as well.

In February of 1863 groups of Confederate soldiers camped near the Rappahannock Academy in Virginia experienced two massive storms that deposited more than seventeen inches of snow on the ground. A friendly snowball fight broke out that soon grew to engulf regiments and ten thousand men in total. Generals planned strategy, raids were undertaken, and prisoners were captured and paroled. The Great Snowball Battle of the Rappahannock Academy became legendary in military history for comical reasons. Yet the idea of actually using weather in warfare is something that nations have tried repeatedly to accomplish.

11

WRITINGS ON WEATHER IN WARFARE

If you know Heaven and you know Earth,
you make your victory complete.
—Sun Tzu

This book opened with the above quote on the influence of nature by one of the greatest military theorists ever. Therefore, it is altogether fitting that it ends with a chapter on the writings of other great strategists that concerned the impact of weather on warfare. The fact that weather and its importance did not escape the most notable of military theorists helps to advance the thesis that the elements were certainly recognized historically as playing a decisive role in combat.

Sun Tzu wrote that, "The art of war, then, is governed by five constant factors."[201] These five elements included some of those more commonly expressed by military writers, including the discipline of the men, the skill of the commander, and having the support of the population. Yet, Sun also includes among these, "heaven," a term he later explains in the following manner: "Heaven signifies night and day, cold and heat, times and seasons."[202] Clearly here Sun is addressing weather, climate, and nature rather than religious influences. The commander who is able to understand heaven, its portents and its phenomenon, was guaranteed victory. Perhaps the most well-known quote from Sun Tzu remains, "If you know the enemy and know yourself, your victory will not stand in doubt."[203] Yet what is often left out is the second half of the statement, "if you know heaven and know earth, you may make your victory complete."

Various Chinese commentators have sought to expand upon Sun's writings, though in the end they have merely reinforced the importance of weather in combat. Li Chuan summarized Sun's famous quote on knowing your enemy as, "Given a knowledge of three things—the affairs of men, the seasons of heaven, and the natural advantages of earth—victory will invariably crown your battles." Another commentator, Chen Hao, placed weather only second to knowing the terrain as the most important factor in combat. Still further, when Sun recommended that, "In order to carry out an attack, we must have means available," Jia Lin explains this as, "We must avail ourselves of wind and dry weather."[204] The importance of wind is especially illustrated by the Battle of Towton in 1461, where the army that was able to position itself with the wind at its back had a natural advantage in projecting its arrows further.

Other Chinese writers, including Sun Bin and Jiang Ziya, also discussed the importance of weather in planning campaigns and undertaking battle. Sun wrote in his recently rediscovered work that, "[In] Warfare . . . man is not the sole factor. You must have the heavenly, earthly, and human advantages: that is weather conditions, terrain, and harmonious troops."[205] At the same time, Jiang Ziya likewise discussed the importance of environmental factors as part of his Tiger Strategy in warfare. Clearly all major ancient Chinese writers on the subject recognized the importance of weather in warfare. Part of this undoubtedly arose from the influence of Daoism upon their thought. This philosophy focused around an appreciation of the natural world and efforts to conform to it.

Publius Flavius Vegetius, in his *De Re Militari*, discusses additional aspects of weather as a force in war. As much of the early part of his book concerns the proper raising and equipping of men for combat, it is not surprising to see a treatment of the aspects of weather and climate. "No one, I imagine, can doubt that the peasants are the most fit to carry arms for they from their infancy have been exposed to all kinds of weather." Two particular elements he addresses which he claims the poorer classes are abler to withstand include, "the sun and dust."[206] The focus of Vegetius is clearly in building an army able to bear the unpredictable elements of weather and nature, rather than attempt to avoid or control them.

Once in the field, Vegetius was quick to remind commanders that care must be taken to properly clothe and house soldiers in order to avoid exposure to the elements. "Preserving the health of the troops . . . depends . . . on the season of the year . . . they will contract diseases from the heat of the weather."[207] Vegetius also cautioned against marching in the snow or moving through a swamp for the same reasons. The miasma theory of disease strongly influenced much of the early thinking about weather and warfare; Vegetius went so far as to caution against exercising men in anything but fine weather.[208] Though one would assume that acclimatizing men to all conditions would be of the utmost importance, for Vegetius the health of the men came first.

The importance of weather and nature re-emerged in the writing of Machiavelli a thousand years later. In the guise of the condottieri Fabrizio Colonna, the author reminds us that one of the most important questions a commander can ask is, "what benefit the weather might give you or take away."[209] Still further, when questioned on whether or not a campaign should be launched in the winter, Fabrizio answered that, "the ancients were wiser and conducted their affairs with more prudence than we do at present . . . Nothing can be more dangerous or indiscreet than for a general to carry on a war in wintertime."[210] The commander went on to state that this largely holds true only for the attacker, as the defender has advantage of shelter, food, and warmth. Fabrizio then mentioned that the Battle of Garigliano in 1503 was a prime example of this type of folly. "The defeat of the French near the

Garigliano in 1503 resulted not so much from the bravery of the Spaniards, as from the rigor of the season."[211]

Maurice de Saxe and Frederick the Great, the giants of eighteenth-century military thought and writing, also appreciated the impact wrought by nature on an army in the field. For de Saxe the bulk of its importance concerned the proper dressing of soldiers. He devoted a considerable section of his *Reveries* to these ideas, arguing for better socks, better boots, and even a preference for helmets over hats. He also advised to direct attention to the length of hair on a soldier, as "once the rainy season has arrived, his head is never dry."[212]

De Saxe also followed the connection between climate and disease, retelling how there once existed "a custom of the Romans by which they prevented the diseases that attack armies with changes of climate"[213] through daily consumption of vinegar. Though admitting he didn't understand the exact science behind it, he was more than willing to accept it due to the preponderance of anecdotal evidence.

Perhaps the most striking feature of his work though, was his thinking on winter combat. In direct contrast to nearly three thousand years of tradition and belief, de Saxe suggested that winter combat should be resorted to more frequently than simply in times of emergency. "Winter need not be feared for troops so much as is commonly believed . . . there are no illnesses to fear, fevers are not prevalent as in summer."[214] In couching his argument in terms of disease, de Saxe contradicted commonly held, though erroneous beliefs correlating winter with illness.

Frederick the Great, based on his own stated experience, disagreed with de Saxe on the topic of winter warfare. "It is only absolute necessity and great advantages which can excuse winter operations. Ordinarily, they ruin the troops because of the sickness by which they are followed."[215] As mentioned previously, erroneous miasma theory largely informed this sentiment emphasizing the spread of illness more than concerns over restriction on movements or supplies. Frederick sought to further convince his generals by suggesting that while they could campaign in the winter, it is more useful to use that time to recruit and train soldiers. Still later, while recounting several times where he was personally forced to campaign in winter, he recommended living off the enemy's lands as much as possible. Overall, he reiterated the now-consistent advice of all previous writers on the subject: "It is always necessary to form projects of campaign, as I have said, on estimates of the weather."

George Washington frequently mentioned the effects of weather in his writings. As early as his time serving in Virginia and Ohio during the French and Indian War, Washington recorded the impact of weather upon his campaigns. "This is a fact nobody here takes upon him to deny. The General and great part of the troops, &c, being yet behind, and the weather growing very inclement, must, I apprehend, terminate our expedition for this year, at this place."[216] While in winter quarters, he went on to relate to the governor of Virginia that, "our men that are left there, are in such a miserable situation, having hardly rags to cover their nakedness, exposed to the inclemency of the weather in this rigorous season, that, unless provision is made by the country for supplying them immediately, they must inevitably perish."[217] In fact Washington was quick to blame the inclement weather for part of the reason why he was forced to surrender Fort Necessity. "They being without shelter, rainy weather, and their trenches to the knee in water, whereas the French were sheltered all round our camp by trees."[218]

Years later, Washington often cited weather as one of the main hardships he faced during the Revolution. As early as 1775, he wrote to the Massachusetts General Assembly, predicting disaster should his army not be supplied with fuel and clothing to fight off the approaching winter. "If there comes a spell of rain or cold weather must inevitably disperse; the consequence of which needs no animadversion of mine."[219] A few days later, he wrote directly to Congress itself requesting the issuance of more ammunition as, "The long series of wet weather, which we have had, renders the greater part of what has been served out to the men of no use."[220] For the rest of the winter Washington frequently commented upon the part that weather played in both delaying the progress of his men in digging entrenchments around Boston as well as slowing the arrival of British reinforcements from Europe and Halifax.

While Napoleon himself did not leave a large collection of writings, Clausewitz's *Art of War* is normally taken to be the best representation of the French general's maxims. He included weather as one of the "chance" elements of war:

> This enormous friction, which is not concentrated, as in mechanics, at a few points, is therefore everywhere brought into contact with chance, and thus incidents take place upon which it was impossible to calculate, their chief origin being chance. As an instance of one such chance: the weather. Here the fog prevents the enemy from being discovered in time, a battery from firing at the right moment, a report from reaching the General; there the rain prevents a battalion from arriving at the right time, because instead of for three it had to march perhaps eight hours; the cavalry from charging effectively because it is stuck fast in heavy ground.[221]

Clausewitz goes on to mention on several occasions in his work the importance of weather as a phenomenon to understand when investigating a region to campaign in, as importance as ground type and time of day.[222] Yet, quite interestingly, the author then goes on to suggest that, "Still more rarely has the weather any decisive influence, and it is mostly only by fogs that it plays a part."[223] Is this due to a failure to explore the history of the subject by Clausewitz? This would seem unlikely due to the fact that, as shown previously, Napoleon's own campaigns were often impacted by weather and nature. More likely, this is in keeping with Clausewitz's general theme that the proper application of resources, thought, and energy by a general can overcome minor issues of weather or terrain.

Helmuth von Moltke, himself an ardent student of Clausewitz and Napoleon, mentioned weather as one of the unknowns of war. "These are fully unforeseeable: weather, illness, railway accidents, misunderstandings, and disappointments—in short, all the influences that one may call luck, fate, or higher providence, which mankind neither creates nor dominates."[224] His statement seems to have followed his own experiences during the Prussian war with Denmark in 1864. "One can base no operations on weather, but one can base them on season."[225]

As late as the twentieth century, Erwin Rommel discussed the role played by fog in his own experiences during World War I. During his first operation of the war, an assault on Bleid, Rommel and his men were forced to deal with heavy ground fog that shrouded the number and movements of the enemy. In his observations on the battle, Rommel recounted that,

> It is difficult to maintain contact in fog. During the battle in the fog at Bleid, contact was lost soon after meeting the enemy, and it was not possible to reestablish it. Advances through fog by means of a compass must be practiced, since smoke will frequently be employed. In a meeting engagement in the fog, the side capable of developing a maximum fire power on contact will get the upper hand; therefore keep the machine guns ready for action at all times during the advance.[226]

Likewise, his book is rife with references to rain, cold temperatures, and snow, as well as the effects that these had on both his men and his missions.

Winston Churchill also recognized the role that the Battle of the Atlantic played in the war effort, specifically the meteorological knowledge supplied by the Coast Guard ships that patrolled the area. "The Battle of the Atlantic was the dominating factor all through the war . . . Never for one moment could we forget that everything happening elsewhere, on land, at sea, or in the air depended ultimately on its outcome."

Interestingly, many of the most notable writers on guerrilla warfare, Mao Zedong, Vo Nguyen Giap, and Che Guevara, largely ignored the topic. The impact of weather on their operations was not discussed in any of their major pieces. Perhaps this was due to the fact that local forces would be more accustomed to these conditions, or weather would not have had such an impact when operating in small numbers on variable schedules. Giap is one of the few that even mentioned weather, but purely in terms of an opportunity to coordinate the army and the peasantry. "Our army has always organized days of help for peasants in production work and in the struggle against flood and drought. It has always observed a correct attitude in its relations with the people."[227]

US Army Field Manual 3–24, *Insurgencies and Countering Insurgencies*, which was released in 2006 and updated in 2014, does mention the factor of weather and climate as it impacts the modern battlefield. Early on in the work it is included as one of the components of the physical dimensions of the information variable that commanders must take into account when planning.

> 2–41. The physical environment includes the geography and man-made structures, as well as the climate and weather, in an area of operations. The physical environment affects the tactics and operations of both insurgents and counterinsurgents. Extreme conditions, such as in nations in higher elevations, can make insurgent movements difficult in the winter. The movement and the tactics of any military force will be affected by the physical environment of its area of operations. A physical environment will influence insurgency sanctuaries, the ability of an insurgency to hide resources, and the ability of an insurgency to mass forces. Understanding a physical environment is essential to understanding an insurgency.[228]

This was especially true for American and allied operations in Afghanistan, where winter conditions would often shut down the vital supply passes from Pakistan.

Overall, military thinkers and leaders have appreciated weather as an important component of military strategy for millennia. Yet, as seen from the vast majority of literature on the topic, it has often not received the focus that its gravity deserves. Part of this certainly arises from its unpredictable nature, especially prior to the twentieth century. With the advent of modern meteorological science and techniques however, weather is becoming a more recognized and appreciated factor in the planning of both wars and national strategy.

CONCLUSION

Thou shalt be visited of the LORD of hosts with thunder,
and with earthquake, and great noise, with storm and
tempest, and the flame of devouring fire.
—ISAIAH, 29:6

JUST AS THE CAUSES OF WAR are varied, so too are the plethora of elements that affect its undertaking and outcome. The outbreak of disease, the availability of proper equipment, and the general esprit de corps of the troops, amongst other factors, all play a significant role in shaping battles and campaigns. Weather, the various forces of nature, and certain heavenly aspects have also substantially impacted military history. The sheer variety of types of weather phenomena and the ways in which they can affect men, animals, equipment, and landscape has made it a substantial force in history.

The study of the connection between these two events, nature and war, has been of interest for thousands of years. This is clearly shown by the close mention of the two in various ancient texts such as the Bible and the Iliad. The Rev. Dr. Michael Jacobs meticulously recorded the various temperatures at different points during the Battle of Gettysburg in 1863. Yet despite all of these mentions and recordings, little has been done to actively glean connections between historical events and weather.

This is all the more interesting today due to both scientific and technological advances as well as recent discussion on anthropogenic climate change. Several modern governments have attempted to construct weapons, or to utilize techniques to harness or simulate the power of nature, as briefly mentioned above. The roots of this lie in traditional religious attempts to do the same. Whereas early man employed prayer and sacrifice to summon rain or avert hurricanes, modern man uses silver iodide and dry ice. Though the harnessing of larger forces such as earthquakes and tidal waves may remain at present in the realm of science fiction, that should not discount their future appearance. In fact, even conventional attacks on dams and dykes, an age-old tactic, was taken up in discussion and banned internationally by Protocol I of the Geneva Convention at a conference in 1977.

The earth's climate has changed periodically and frequently since the planet's formation. Even within man's short tenure on the planet a number of factors have led to marked change in both weather patterns and temperatures. Historical warming trends have been associated with the rise of the Roman Empire, while periods of global cooling are associated with the Dark Ages in Europe and the downfall of the Maya and Teotihuacan in the Americas. A more specific example occurred over the winter of 1241 to 1242 when warming temperatures as part of a localized climate change led to melting snow in the Carpathian Mountains and increased rainfall. This coincided with the Mongol incursion into central Europe. It appears that the resulting excessively marshy grasslands helped to convince the invaders to withdraw as their mounted army found it difficult to maneuver and find food. Despite their tremendous victory the year before at Mohi and the deaths of up to 20 percent of the Hungarian population, the Mongol army turned back toward Russia.[229] Europe was saved due to localized climate change and warming.

Recent conversation on the global stage of the possibility of modern climate change has been paralleled by discussions within military circles. Understanding the effects of weather patterns and temperature extremes on both men and equipment is of vital importance in the planning of campaigns. Likewise, shifting shorelines or receding ice caps, regardless of whether they have natural or anthropogenic causes, would open up new lines of communication and potential invasion routes, alter preexisting defensive perimeters, and require the remapping of regions and coastlines.

In early 2016, the White House announced that the United States military would now focus on climate change as a factor in combat. The Pentagon summarized this as the "ability to anticipate, prepare for, and adapt to changing conditions and withstand, respond to, and recover rapidly from disruptions."[230] The directive applies broadly to almost every area of military life and planning, including the purchasing of weapons systems and troop training. Though opponents labeled this move as largely political and partisan in nature, the idea that any elements of weather, temperature, and extremes of nature could affect military operations is a historical truth and not a recent development.

Quite interestingly as well, the connection has also been proposed previously but in an opposite direction. In 1890, Edward Powers wrote a book in which he sought to establish a connection between the vast amount of explosives used in the Civil War and increased rainfall afterward. Entitled *War and the Weather*, the book convinced Congress to spend $10,000 to experiment on whether or not the proposition was true. Several decades later, Alexander McAdie proposed the same connection regarding the battles of the Great War in *The Atlantic*. Though the evidence presented was circumstantial and the thesis weak, the idea does present another interesting take on the reverse connection between weather and warfare.[231]

A similar study has studied the effect of air warfare on the local climate of England. The hundreds to thousands of planes that took off each day from fields in England during World War II produced vast numbers of contrails and amounts of water vapor in the atmosphere. A study performed in 2011 at the Lancaster Environment Centre has determined that on May 11, 1944, alone, following the launching of over 1,440 aircraft toward Germany, local temperatures were depressed. While the effect was certainly localized and temporary, there is a potential for it to apply to modern air travel if extrapolated.[232]

Overall, several truisms emerge from the study of weather and warfare. Combat in all of its forms, on land, at sea, and in the air, are affected by weather. Though technology has mitigated some of these interactions, especially in the air and at sea, the unexpected can still occur. On land, weather can serve to limit movement, foul equipment, and spread death, disease, and injury. On the macro level, adverse weather can damage a nation and its economy and infrastructure to a point that seriously impedes its military capability. Finally, the connection between nature and warfare is far from an archaic occurrence. Recent wars have shown that while some elements of weather can be predicted or mitigated through science and technology, it cannot always be avoided. In fact, in many cases, more modern, sensitive equipment can be even more susceptible to environmental interference.

Oscar Wilde once opined that, "conversation about the weather is the last refuge of the unimaginative." Clearly he meant that dull and meandering talk for which there is no connection to other ideas or loftier goals than just passing time. But if one were to examine the impact of that weather on economics, art, society, politics, or in the case of our present volume, military history, they would see a fascinating and altogether important topic, one that should be discussed more often especially in military circles. As Shakespeare himself wrote, "When clouds appear, wise men put on their cloaks."[233]

INDEX

NOTES

1   Hesiod, *Theogony*, Lines 687–712.

2   Ibid., 821–835.

3   Ibid., 844–849.

4   *Mahabharata*, Book VI, Section III, Lines 9–12.

5   Pliny, *Natural History*, Book II, XXII, 89–90.

6   Ibid., II, XXIII.

7   *Mahabharata,* Book VI, Section III, Line 12.

8   Ibid., II, XXII, 89–90.

9   George Smith, *The History of Babylon* (New York: Pott, Young, & Co., 1877), 96.

10   J.L. Brady, "Halley's Comet: AD 1986 to 2647 BC," *Journal of the British Astronomical Association* 92, No. 5 (1982): 209–215.

11   Pliny, 89–90.

12   Noah Webster, *A Brief History of Epidemic and Pestilential Disease*, Vol. 1 (Hartford: Hudson and Goodwin, 1799), 33.

13   Aristotle, *Meteorology*, Book I, Chapter 6, Lines 35–36.

14   Plutarch, *Life of Lysander.*

15   Daniel Graham, "An Ancient Greek Sighting of Halley's Comet?," *Journal of Cosmology* 9 (2010): 2130–2136.

16   Plutarch, *Life of Lysander.*

17   A dagger discovered in the tomb of Tutankhamun has recently been determined to be of meteoric origin.

18   Ibid.

19   *Iliad*, Book XIX.

20   Pliny, Book II, XXV.

21   Livy, *History of Rome*, Book XXI, 1.

22   Ibid., Book XXIX, 10.

23   Ibid., 11.

24   Justinus 37.2.1.

25   Ovid, *Metamorphosis*, Book XV, 745–746.

26   Ibid., 745–842.

27   Nandini Pandey, "Caesar's Comet, the Julian Star, and the Invention of Augustus," *Transactions of the American Philological Association* 143 (2013): 405–449.

28   Cassius Dio, *History of Rome*, 41, 14, 3.

29   Pliny, Book II, XXV.

30   Flavius Josephus, *The Wars of the Jews*, Book VI, 288.

31   Eusebius Pamphilius, *The Life of Constantine,* Book I, Chapter XXVIII.

32   Ibid., Chapter XXXI.

33   Y.N. Chin and H. L. Huang, "Identification of the Guest Star of 185 as a Comet Rather Than a Supernova," *Nature* 371 (1994): 398–399.

34   Theodricus Monachus, *De antiquitate regum Norwagiensium*, Ian McDougall, trans. (London: Viking Society, 1998), Chapter 28.

35   Herodotus, *The Histories*, Book I, 73–74.

36   Ibid., Book VII, 37.

37   W. T. Lynn, "Eclipses during the war of Xerxes against the Greeks," *The Observatory* 7 (April 18, 1884): 138–140.

38   Herodotus, Book VII, 38.

39   Thucydides, *History of the Peloponnesian War*, Book VII.

40   Plutarch, *Lives* (Baltimore: William and Joseph Neal, 1836), 478.

41   Plutarch, *Life of L. Aemilius Paulus.*

42   Holinshed.

43   William Walker Canfield, *The Legends of the Iroquois: Told by the Cornplanter* (New York: A. Wessels Co, 1904), 36–37.

44   Bruce E. Johansen, "Dating the Iroquois Confederacy," *Akwesasne Notes, New Series* 1, no. 3 and 4 (Fall 1995): 62–63.

45   William Least, *Heat Moon, Columbus in the Americas* (New York: John Wiley and Sons, 2002), 175.

46 Bertrand Mitford, *Through the Zulu Country* (London: Keegan, Paul, Trench & Co., 1883), 95.

47 "A War-Eclipse Cartoon," *NY Times*, Aug. 22, 1914.

48 *Wheeling Daily Intelligence* (Sept. 3, 1859).

49 Delores J. Knipp, "1967 Solar Storm Nearly Took Us to Brink of War," *American Geophysical Union*, Aug. 9, 2016.

50 2 Kings 19: 35–36.

51 See William H. McNeill, "Infectious Alternatives," in Robert Cowley, ed., *What If?* (New York: G.P. Putnam and Sons, 1999).

52 Marcus Junianus Justinus, *Epitome of the Philippic History of Pompeius Trogus*, trans. by John Selby Watson (London: Henry G. Bohn, 1835) Book II, Section XI.

53 Livy, *History of Rome*, Book V, Section XLVII.

54 Appian, *The Civil Wars*, Book I, Paragraph 89.

55 Ibid., 93.

56 Stephen Turnbull, *The Samurai Sourcebook* (London: Cassell and Company, 2000), 201.

57 Radu Florescu, *Dracula: Prince of Many Faces: His Life and Times* (Boston: Little, Brown, and Company, 1989), 145.

58 See Alfred Toppe, *Night Combat* (Washington, DC: Center of Military History, 1986).

59 "Moon Stirs Scare of Missile Launch," *NY Times*, Dec. 7, 1960.

60 *Mahabharata*, trans. by William Buck (Berkeley: University of California Press, 2000), 39.

61 *Iliad*, Book XII, 25.

62 Ibid., Book XVI, 384–392.

63 Paul Simons, "Weather Eye," *The Times of London* (April 3, 2014).

64 Judges 4:14–15.

65 Judges 5:21 and Flavius Josephus, *Antiquities of the Jews*, Book V, Chapter 5, Paragraph 4.

66 Herodotus, Book VI, Chapter 44, Sections 2–3.

67 Ibid., Book VII, Chapters 188–190.

68 Ibid., Book VIII, Chapter 13.

69 Thucydides, *History of the Peloponnesian War*, Book III, Section 22–23.

70 Appian, Book I, Paragraph 90.

71   Cassius Dio, *History of Rome*, Book 72, Chapter 8 published in Vol. IX of the Loeb Classical Library edition, 1927.

72   Ibid., Chapter 9.

73   George Roberts, *The Life, Progress, and Rebellion of James, Duke of Monmouth*, Vol. II (London: Longman, 1844), 35.

74   Anne Curry, *The Battle of Agincourt: Sources and Interpretations* (Woodbridge: Boydell Press, 2000), 106.

75   Washington Irving, *Chronicle of the Conquest of Granada* (Philadelphia: J.B. Lippincott and Company, 1872), 486–487.

76   Garcia de Resende, "Life and Times of King John II".

77   *The Westminster Review,* Vol. 26 (London: Henry Hooper, 1837), 566.

78   David R. Petriello, *Bacteria and Bayonets: Disease in American Military History* (Philadelphia: Casemate, 2015), 122–126.

79   George Washington to The President of Congress, Letter (August 29, 1776).

80   Quoted by Richard Bentley, "Weather in Wartime," *Quarterly Journal of the Royal Meteorological Society* 33–34 (1907): 89.

81   Edward P.F. Rose, "The Battle of Waterloo, 18 June 1815: Some Geological Reflections to Mark the Bicentenary," *Geology Today* 31, no. 3 (May-June 2015): 106–107.

82   Allan Nevins, ed., *A Diary of Battle: The Personal Journals of Col. Charles S. Wainwright* (New York: De Capo Press, 1998), 158.

83   Eric Ethier, "Folly at Mill Springs," *America's Civil War* 28, no. 5 (Nov. 2015): 49.

84   "The Battle of Sadowa," *Chicago Tribune* (July25, 1866).

85   Capt. Henry Brackenbury, *The Ashanti War (1874) Volume 2: A Narrative* (London: Andrews, 2012), 205.

86   Frances Ellen Colenso, *History of the Zulu War and its Origin* (London: Chapman and Hall, 1880), 378.

87   Alexander Wilmot, *History of the Zulu War* (London: Richardson, 1880), 175.

88   Charles F. Brooks, "World-Wide Changes of Temperature," *Geographical Review* 2, no. 4 (Oct. 1916): 249–255.

89   B. Liddell Hart, *Strategy* (London: Meridian Books, 1967), 203–204.

90   John J. Tolson, *Airmobility: 1961–1971* (Washington: Department of the Army, 1999), 192.

91   Clausewitz, *On War.*

92   Exodus 13:19–20.

93   John Timbs, *Abbeys, Castles and Ancient Balls of England and Wales, Their Legendary Lore, and Popular History* (London: Frederick Warne and Co, 1872), 151.

94   *The Campaign of 1776 Around New York and Brooklyn,* Memoirs of the Long Island Historical Society, Vol. III (Brooklyn: LIHS, 1878), 223.

95   Georges Blond, *The Grand Army,* 70.

96   "Paul von Hindenburg on the Opening of the German Spring Offensive," in *Source Records of the Great War, Vol. VI,* ed. Charles F. Horne (National Alumni, 1923).

97   Marvin D. Kays, "Weather Effects During the Battle of the Bulge and the Normandy Invasion," US Army Electronics Research and Development Command: Atmospheric Sciences Laboratory, Aug. 1982.

98   Ashley Fantz, "Under the Cover of Fog, the Kurds Battle ISIS," *CNN,* Dec. 7, 2015, http://www.cnn.com/2015/12/07/world/syria-kurdish-fighters-isis-battle/.

99   Bradley Graham, "Kosovo Campaign Dwarfed by Gulf War," *Washington Post*, April 2, 1999.

100   Exodus 14: 21–22.

101   Francois-Marie Voltaire, *History of Charles XII, King of Sweden* (London, 1908), 305.

102   Herodotus, Book VI, Chapter 66, Sections 2.

103   George Cawkwell, *Philip of Macedon* (London: Faber & Faber, 1978), 74.

104   Ibid., Book VII, Chapter 178.

105   Ibid., Chapters 188–189.

106   Plutarch, *Life of Themistocles.*

107   Diodorus Siculus, Book XI, Chapter 20.

108   Polybius, *The General History of Polybius,* Book I, 25.

109   Ambrose of Milan, *De Obitu Theodosii*, 10.

110   Quran 8:17.

111   Dunois (II, 16) as quoted in Regine Pernoud, *Joan of Arc: Her Story* (New York: Palgrave, 1999), 40.

112   Gilbert Burnet, *History of My Own Time*, Vol. III (London: A. Millar, 1753), 252.

113   Comte de Forbin.

114 Catherine Drinker Bowen, *John Adams and the American Revolution* (Boston: Little, Brown, and Company, 1951), 10–11.

115 Alfred Thayer Mahan, *The Influence of Sea Power Upon History* (Boston: Little Brown and Company, 1890), 304.

116 Cuthbert Collingwood to the Admiralty (Nov. 1805), in Nicholas Tracy, *Nelson's Battles: The Triumph of British Seapower* (Washington: Naval Institute Press, 2008), 249.

117 "Reflections and Extracts from the Journal of Miss Anne Prevost," (June 3, 1813).

118 Despite these developments, the Battle of the Denmark Strait in May of 1941 saw a British squadron hampered by the German gaining of the weather gauge. In the end the *HMS Hood* was sunk and over fourteen hundred lives were lost.

119 M. Chenowith, "Hurricane Amanda: Rediscovery of a Forgotten US Civil War Florida Hurricane," *American Meteorological Society* (Nov. 2013): 1735–1742.

120 Charles D. Ross, "Outdoor Sound Propagation in the US Civil War," *Echoes* 9, no. 1 (Winter 1999): 1–5.

121 The Japanese Fourth Fleet suffered significant loss in 1935 during a typhoon in the Pacific. Major design flaws were revealed in their ships which were largely remedied before WWII.

122 B.C. Goss, "An Artillery Gas Attack," *The Journal of Industrial and Engineering Chemistry* 11 (September 1919): 831.

123 Roger Barr, "The Pittsburgh's Typhoon Battle," *Naval History* 29, no. 5 (Oct. 2015).

124 Jack Williams, "How Typhoons at the end of World War II Swamped U.S. Ships and Nearly Saved Japan from Defeat," *Washington Post*, July 16, 2015.

125 Kelly Kennedy, "Study: Wind Blew Deadly Gas to U.S. Troops in Gulf War," *USA Today*, Dec. 14, 2012.

126 Joshua 10:11.

127 C.L. Kingsford (ed.), *Chronicles of London* (Oxford, 1905), 13.

128 "Hail Cannons of France," *Southland Times* 30, no. 19676 (Sept. 30, 1905).

129 "Hardships in the Snow," from Xenophon's *Anabasis*, in C.D. Warner, et al., *The Library of the World's Best Literature. An Anthology in Thirty Volumes* (1917).

130 Ibid.

131 See Shane Brennan, "Mind the Gap: A Snow Lacuna in Xenophon's Anabasis?," in *Xenophon: Ethical Principles and Historical Enquiry* (Brill, 2012), 307–339.

132 Polybius, Book III, 54.

133 Ibid., III, 74.

134 Edward Gibbon, *The History of the Decline and Fall of the Roman Empire*, Chapter 36, Line 47.

135 Jon Latimer, "Storm of Snow and Steel at Narva," *Military History* 17, no. 5 (Dec. 2000): 62.

136 Thomas Carlyle, *History of Friedrich II*, Chapter X.

137 Thomas Campbell, "Hohenlinden."

138 David Schimmelpenninck van der Oye, "Paul's Great Game: Russia's Plan to Invade British India," *Central Asian Survey* 33, no. 2 (2014): 149–150.

139 Col. George Veith as quoted in Graydon Tunstall, "The Carpathian Winter War, 1915," *MHQ Magazine*, May 13, 2014.

140 Quintus Curtius Rufus, *History of Alexander the Great of Macedonia*, 7.5.1–16.

141 Dio Cassius, *Roman History*, LIII.29.3–8.

142 "A Roman Experience with Heat Stroke in 24 B.C.," *Bulletin of the New York Academy of Medicine* 43 no. 8. (1967):767–768.

143 Plutarch, *The Life of Marius*, 26, trans. by John Dryden.

144 *The Old French Continuation of William of Tyre*, Chapters 40–41.

145 Ibid., Chapter 41.

146 From Sihab al-Din bin Fadl Allah al-'Umar, *Masalik al-absar fi mamalik*.

147 The subsequent Siege of Limerick dragged on due to the onset of winter and eventually saw William return to the comforts of London.

148 Peter O. Koch, *The Aztecs, the Conquistadors, and the Making of Mexican Culture* (New York: McFarland, 2005), 165–166.

149 David R. Petriello, *Bacteria and Bayonets: The Impact of Disease Upon American Military History* (Philadelphia: Casemate, 2016), 136.

150 Jon Latimer, "The Second Sikh War," *Military History* 23, no. 9 (Dec. 2006).

151 Geoffrey Hunt, *Colorado's Volunteer Infantry in the Philippine Wars, 1898–1899* (2006), 193.

152 Alexander Watson, *Ring of Steel: Germany and Austria-Hungary in World War I* (2014), 126.

153 Douglas Casa, et al., "Historical Perspectives on Medical Care for Heat Stroke, Part 2," *Athletic Training and Sports Healthcare* 2, no. 4 (2010): 183.

154 Livy, Book XXI, 54–55.

155 Ibid., 56.

156 Quran, 33:9.

157 Frederick Schiller, *History of the Thirty Year's War* (New York: Harper and Brothers, 1846), 345.

158 George Washington to the President of Congress, Letter (Feb. 18, 1776).

159 George Washington to the President of Congress, Letter (Dec. 23, 1777).

160 Adolphe Thiers, *History of the Consulate and the Empire of France Under Napoleon* (Paris: H. Colburn, 1845), 146.

161 Quoted by Bentley, 96.

162 E.A. FitzGerald, *The Highest Andes* (New York: Scribner's Sons, 1899), 31.

163 H. Killian, *Cold and Frost Injuries — Rewarming Damages Biological, Angiological, and Clinical Aspects: Biological, Angiological, and Clinical Aspects* (Springer Science and Business, 2012), appendix.

164 R. L. Atenstaedt, "Trench Foot: The Medical Response in the First World War," *Wilderness Environmental Medicine* 17, no. 4 (Winter 2006): 282–289.

165 Gerald Astor, *A Blood-Dimmed Tide, The Battle of the Bulge by the Men Who Fought It* (Donald I. Fine Inc., 1992), 258.

166 "Two Letters from a British soldier in the British North Russian Expeditionary Force," in *The Workers' Dreadnought* (1919).

167 Karl Warner, "Combating Cold in Korea," (US Army Heritage and Education Center, Nov. 10, 2010).

168 Adele Slaughter, "Korean vets reveal cold truth about skin cancer," *USA Today*, May 25, 2001.

169 Book of Exodus, 14:26–28.

170 Rig Veda, Book VII, Hymn XVIII.

171 Polybius, *Histories*, Book III, 79.

172 Roff Smith, "Drought Led to Collapse of Civilizations, Study Says," *National Geographic*, Oct. 25, 2013.

173 Lawrence G. Kautz, *August Valentine Kautz: Biography of a Civil War General* (New York: McFarland, 2015), 144.

174   Stuart W. Sanders, "Carnage in Kentucky's Hills," *Civil War Times* 51, no. 5 (Oct. 2012).

175   Daniel Davis, "A Near Disaster: The Wilson-Kautz Raid," *Civil War Times* 55, no. 1 (Feb. 2016).

176   Heinz Guderian, *Memories of a Soldier* (Heidelberg: Vowinckel, 1951), 354–355.

177   Thucydides, Book III.

178   Livy, *The History of Rome*, Book 22, Chapter 5, Line 8.

179   Raymond d'Aguilers from August. C. Krey, *The First Crusade: The Accounts of Eyewitnesses and Participants* (Princeton: Princeton University Press, 1921), 139–142.

180   Book of Joshua, 6:15–20.

181   William J. Broad, "It Swallowed a Civilization," *New York Times*, Oct. 21, 2003, D1.

182   "Intrepid Cruiser Philadelphia Ran from Volcano," *Sun*, Nov. 7, 1944.

183   Herodotus, 3.26.

184   As recounted in Khalid Yahya Blankinship trans., *The History of Al-Tabari: The Challenge to the Empires* (New York: SUNY Press, 1993).

185   Plutarch, *The Life of Marius*, 26, trans. by John Dryden.

186   John W. Anderson, "An Analysis of a Dust Storm Impacting Operation Iraqi Freedom, 25–27 March 2003" MA diss., Naval Postgraduate School, 82.

187   Ibid., 86.

188   Pausanias, *Description of Greece*, Book X, Chapter 23, Paragraph 1.

189   Justinus, Epitome to Pompeius Trogus's *Philippic Histories*, Book 24, Chapter 8.

190   Xenophon, *Cyrus the Great: The Arts of Leadership and War*, ed. Larry Hedrick (New York: St. Marten's Press, 2006), 55.

191   Herodotus Book 1, Chapter 191.

192   Thucydides, Book 5, Chapter 65.

193   Plutarch, *The Life of Camillus*, trans. by John Dryden.

194   *Life of Marius*, 26.

195   John L. Tone, *The Fatal Knot: The Guerrilla War in Navarre and the Defeat of Napoleon in Spain* (Charlotte: UNC Press, 1994), 43–44.

196   This unit provided the accurate explanations in 1967 that prevented a nuclear strike against Russia when the nation's BMEWS went out during a solar storm.

197 Richard A. Gabriel, *The Ancient World* (Greenwood Publishing Group, 2007), 40–41.

198 Danny S. Parker, *The Battle of the Bulge* (De Capo Press, 2004), 309.

199 William S. Cohen, "Speech at the Conference on Terrorism, Weapons of Mass Destruction, and U.S. Strategy at the University of Georgia," April 28, 1997.

200 Brain Todd, "U.S. Had Plans to Nuke Moon," *CNN*, Nov. 28, 2012.

201 Sun Tzu, *The Art of War*, I, 3–4.

202 Ibid., I, 7.

203 Ibid., I, 31.

204 Ibid., XII, 2.

205 Sun Bin, *The Art of Warfare*, Chapter VI, trans. D.C. Lau (SUNY Press, 2003), 112.

206 Vegetius, *De Re Militari*, Book I.

207 Ibid., Book III.

208 Ibid.

209 Niccolo Machiavelli, *The Art of War*, Book VI.

210 Ibid.

211 Ibid.

212 Maurice de Saxe, *My Reveries*.

213 Ibid.

214 Ibid.

215 Frederick the Great, *Military Instructions to His Generals*, Article XXVIII.

216 George Washington to Governor Fauquier, Letter (Oct. 30, 1758).

217 Ibid., (Dec. 2, 1758).

218 George Washington to Governor Dinwiddie, Letter (June 12, 1754).

219 George Washington to the Mass. General Court, Letter (Nov. 2, 1775).

220 George Washington to The President of Congress, Letter (Nov. 11, 1775).

221 Carl von Clausewitz, *Art of War*, Book I, Chapter VII.

222 Ibid., Book II, Chapter II, Sections 30 and 35.

223 Ibid., Section 33.

224 Helmuth von Moltke, "On Strategy" (1871), in Daniel Hughes, *Moltke on the Art of War* (New York: Random House, 2009).

225 Helmuth von Moltke, "Military Works".

226 Erwin Rommel, *Infantry Attacks*.

227 Vo Nguyen Giap, "People's War, People's Army," (1959).

228 US Army Field Manuel 3–24, Chapter 2, Section 41.

229 Ulf Buntgen, "Climatic and environmental aspects of the Mongol withdrawal from Hungary in 1242 CE," *Scientific Reports* 6 (2016).

230 Rowan Scarborough, "Pentagon orders commanders to prioritize climate change in all military actions," *Washington Times*, Feb. 7, 2016.

231 Alexander McAdie, "Has the War Affected the Weather?" *The Atlantic,* Sept. 1916.

232 Rob Mackenzie, "Wartime Weather Records Reveal Impact of Contrails Caused by USAAF Raids," *International Journal of Climatology* (2011).

233 William Shakespeare, *Richard III*, Act II, Scene III.